Testing
Your Grammar

Revised Edition

This is Ludger's 'Grammar Study Book', bought
by Ms. Robecca Chorié Lee, who is always complaining about his bad grammar and minor conversation abilities. Ludger promises herowith, that he
will study English grammar now, i.e. at least one

Testing
Your Grammar
Revised Edition

..our per day in order to become a good American,
..likeable fellow and a good and trustful and

Susan M. Reinhart

reliable husband, jaja!

Chicago, Illinois
May 25, 2005

Ann Arbor

THE UNIVERSITY OF MICHIGAN PRESS

He will study the mostest!

To my mother and father

Ludger Roedder
05/05
Chicago, IL

Acknowledgments

I am grateful to the following people for their contributions to the first edition of this text: John Haugen, Taco Homburg, Devon Woods, and Paula Goodfellow commented on parts of the manuscript and provided insights into testing in general; Karen Adams reviewed the manuscript and suggested important changes and additions; and a number of my students significantly improved the manuscript by asking a lot of questions and offering helpful comments.

For help with the second edition, I especially wish to thank my colleagues at the English Language Institute, University of Michigan, for providing a stimulating and supportive work environment. Thanks in particular to Brenda Imber for keeping me company in the North University Building in the evenings and on weekends. My special thanks to Chris Feak, who has not only inspired me professionally over the years but has also solved my computer problems more times than I can count.

I am indebted to two special people at the University of Michigan Press: Kelly Sippell, for mostly saying yes, and Chris Milton, who, along with Kelly, has worked endless hours on my texts.

Finally, I would like to express my deepest appreciation to Dr. John Bordie of the University of Texas at Austin, who some years ago encouraged my first attempts at materials development. I will always be grateful for his support.

Contents

Introduction

Testing Your Grammar was written for high-intermediate and advanced students of English as a second language. The text was first envisioned as a series of practice grammar tests for students taking English language proficiency exams. In the end, however, it developed into a far more comprehensive review of grammatical structures of English. The text covers major aspects of English grammar, including count and noncount nouns, agreement, verb tense, modals, comparisons, and complex clauses, that students need to manage in order to improve their proficiency in English. Each unit contains an explanation of the grammar points presented and a number of exercises to help students monitor their progress.

For this new edition, *Testing Your Grammar* has undergone many changes. Some of the units have been enlarged or significantly modified. Mistakes in the text have been corrected and explanations reworked so that they are clearer and easier to read. Examples have been added. The order of some of the units has been changed to improve the flow of the text. Students wrote to request that explanations be included in the answer key. These have been added.

There are eighteen grammar units in *Testing Your Grammar*. The basic format of each unit remains unchanged. First, there is a brief *pretest*. By means of the pretest, students can start to assess their control of the grammar points covered in the unit. The pretest is followed by a grammar *explanation*. Some of the units have more extensive explanations than others, but in general the goal of this text is to summarize information as succinctly as possible, using basic, uncomplicated terminology and omitting points that students are already expected to know as well as minute details and subtle nuances in grammar that are not a priority for learners at this level of English. *Exercises* that follow the explanation provide practice on the points discussed in the unit. A *final test* at the end of each unit, except for unit 11, helps students evaluate their strengths and weaknesses.

A *review test* is found at the end of every two units. It is a quick review of some of the materials in the two preceding units as well as in other prior units. These tests can be given as they appear in the text or used later in the course as part of a general review. Following unit 18, there are four *examinations* for either pre- or posttesting. An *answer key* with explanations is provided at the end of the text.

Units do not need to be used in order, and instructors are encouraged to rearrange them to suit their individual needs. However, if units are rearranged, *review tests* may have to be postponed.

There are two main item types in the text. The first is **multiple choice.** In some exercises, students must choose between two possible answers; in others, they must choose among four. The latter is more representative of standardized tests, but the former is practical because the incorrect choices that are supplied illustrate typical student errors. The second type is **error recognition.** In some exercises, students must decide if the italicized portion of a sentence is correct. In other exercises, students must choose from four italicized portions of a sentence the portion that is incorrect. The latter is more typical of standardized tests. However, the former allows the students to more quickly discover and clarify uncertainties they have about a particular grammar point.

Testing Your Grammar is most effectively used in a classroom with teacher supervision. Checking answers to the *pretest* in class leads into a discussion of the various points in the unit. Grammar explanations, questions, and additional examples from the instructor and the students make for a lively class hour. Instructors can slow down or quicken the pace of the class as necessary. Specific exercises can be done in small groups, giving students the opportunity to explain and defend their choices to other students. Homework can be checked, and additional feedback and practice material can be provided by the teacher. Teachers can explain differences in conversational and academic or formal English, and they can consult grammar reference books for more in-depth discussion of any grammar point.

This having been said, it is possible for individual students to work through part or all of *Testing Your Grammar* on their own. For this reason the answer key with explanations is provided at the end of the text. The pages of the text are perforated so that the answer key can be removed.

Testing Your Grammar does not provide students with task-based or other grammatically based speaking and writing activities. Teachers are encouraged to supplement the text with their own materials in order to help them meet the objectives of their particular course.

Unit 1

Nouns

— Count and Noncount Nouns —

Pretest

Circle the best answer.

1. Do college instructors in the United States give (much homework) (many homeworks)?
2. I'm sorry, but I don't have (much knowledge) (many knowledges) about this type of computer.
3. Do you have (a cup of sugar) (some sugars) I could borrow?
4. (How many) (How much) money do we need for the weekend?
5. Excuse me. Can you give us (a little) (a few) hamburgers?
6. This year the institute is doing (much more research) (many more researches) on academic idioms.
7. (Less) (Fewer) people enroll in swimming classes during the winter.
8. (A large number) (A large amount) of clothes have been sent to the hurricane victims.
9. You're taking (much too much) (much too many) baggage on this vacation.
10. (How many of) (How many) tomatoes are in a pound?

Explanation

Contrasting Count and Noncount Nouns

In English nouns function as either *count* or *noncount* (mass). While some nouns are considered to be count and others noncount, there are many cases where a noun can be count or noncount, depending on how it is used in the sentence. Consider the following pairs of examples.

> Jane went to buy *a hamburger.* (count)
> Jane went to buy *some hamburger.* (noncount)

> At fifty, Aunt Katherine didn't have even *one gray hair.* (count)
> A man with *gray hair* entered the room. (noncount)

In the first sentence, *hamburger* is used as a count noun to refer to a piece of meat between slices of bread. In the second sentence, *hamburger,* a noncount noun, refers to a kind of meat (like lamb, chicken, pork, or fish) that Jane is buying. It is possible to say, *A hamburger* (count) is made from *hamburger* (noncount).

In the third sentence, *hair* is count because the emphasis is on the *number* of gray hairs. However, *hair* is much more commonly viewed as noncount, as in the fourth sentence, which refers to the color of the man's hair.

Count nouns are thought of as more specific entities. The speaker tends to view them as individual, separate units. Noncount or mass nouns, on the other hand, are thought to be more nonspecific, more abstract, or in some cases less tangible. They are not considered easily divisible into individual units. Noncount nouns may include larger masses of things, gases, liquids, granular or powderlike substances, concepts, forces, categories, etc.

The following is a list of count and noncount nouns. Add your own examples.

Noncount	*Count*
homework	an assignment
money	one dollar and fifty cents
gold	a gold bar (*bar* is count)
fruit	an apple, a banana
equipment	a ball and a bat
furniture	a chair, a lamp
clothing	clothes (plural),* a dress
trouble	a problem
news	a news item (*item* is count)
luggage, baggage	a bag, a suitcase
wood	a log, a board, a piece of wood (*piece* is count)
meat:	
pork	a pig, a pork chop
beef	a cow, a hamburger
chicken	a chicken, a chicken leg
coffee	a cup of coffee (*cup* is count)
perfume	a bottle of perfume (*bottle* is count)
knowledge	a piece of knowledge, a fact
information	a piece of information, a bit of information (*bit* is count)
mathematics, biology, psychology	a subject, an area of studies, a major
research	a research paper

*Clothes can be used with quantity expressions such as *a few clothes* but not with numbers. It is generally incorrect to say *two clothes.*

Notice that noncount nouns commonly represent a general class or category of things, such as furniture. Items in that class are usually count, such as *sofa, chair,* and *table.*

Quantity Expressions

Some quantity expressions are used only with noncount nouns, while others are used with count nouns. *Some* and *a lot of* can accompany both.

Noncount	*Count*
a little	a few
little (so little)	few (so few)
less	fewer
much (so much, very much, too much, much too much)	many (so many, very many, too many)
some	some
a lot of	a lot of
an amount of*	a number of

An amount of + a count noun may be used in conversational English, but it is usually avoided in formal English.

Examples of these quantity expressions with count and noncount nouns are

> *So few people* have time to relax. (count)
> I prefer to travel with *less luggage.* (noncount)

The first five quantity expressions in the list cannot be accompanied by *of* if a noun directly follows.

> Can I borrow a little ~~of~~ sugar?
> There are too many ~~of~~ cars on the highway.

Of is used when the speaker is referring to a specific, known entity—a person, a tangible or intangible item, a substance, etc. In these cases, *of* is followed by the definite article *the* or the demonstrative *this,* an object pronoun (e.g., *them, us*), or a possessive pronoun (e.g., *my, his*).

> Some *of the* sugar spilled on the floor.
> John noticed the books on sale and bought a few *of them.*
> A few *of my friends* are pilots.

Practice

Exercise

Circle the letter of the best answer.

1. _____ has just arrived.

   a. A piece of new equipments
   b. A few new equipments
   c. A large number of new equipment
   d. A lot of new equipment

2. _____ tornadoes occurred this year than last year.

   a. Less of
   b. There were less
   c. Fewer
   d. Fewer of

3. I don't hear _____ news from Sophia these days.

   a. many   c. a lot
   b. much   d. much of

4. "Are you going hunting this year?"

   "I don't know. There seem to be _____ deer in this area."

   a. so few   c. not much
   b. so little   d. only a few of

5. "Are you sure you don't want to go to the movies tonight?"

   "I can't. I have _____ ."

   a. too many homeworks   c. much too many homework
   b. much too much homework   d. too much homework assignments

6. "Do you know a town near here called Marshall?"

   "I do, but _____ people have ever heard of it."

   a. few   c. few of
   b. a few   d. not much

7. I'm sorry I'm late. I hope I didn't cause you _____ .

   a. too much problems   c. many trouble
   b. a lot of problem   d. too much trouble

8. "The price of chocolate has really gone up."

   "Yes. They give you _____ for your money now."

   a. so few   c. so little
   b. so less   d. fewer

9. "_____ do you think we need?"

   "Oh, about a gallon."

   a. How many paint   c. How much paint
   b. How much of paint   d. How many paints

10. "I'm looking for something to eat."

    "There's _____ meat in the refrigerator."

    a. a little of   c. a few
    b. a little   d. few

11. I've never seen _____ people at a soccer game.

    a. so many   c. so much of
    b. so much   d. so many of

12. "What would you like to drink?"

"I'll have _____ , please."

a. a coffee cup
b. small coffee

~~c.~~ a little coffee
d. a few coffee

13. Hector wasn't able to give us _____ information.

~~a.~~ much
b. any of

c. many
d. a lot

14. _____ fish arc in that fish tank?

a. How much
~~b.~~ How many

c. How much of the
d. How much of

15. _____ do we need for the winter?

a. How many woods
b. How many wood

c. How much of wood
~~d.~~ How much wood

— Articles *a, an,* and *the:* Singular versus Plural —

Pretest

Study the following sentences. Decide if the italicized portion of the sentence is *correct* (C) or *incorrect* (I). Circle your answer.

1. We arc looking for *an* information about apartments for rent. C (I)
2. Many years ago this coastal tribe developed *importants* methods of fishing that are still used today. C (I)
3. Usually *childrens* begin to take an interest in reading around the age of five. C (I)
4. The contestants who arc taking part in the 300 *meter* race come from various sections of the city. (C) I
5. It takes *a* hour or two to get to the Mexican border from San Antonio. C (I)
6. Every *people* who has eaten at the new restaurant says it's good. C (I)
7. You must complete work on *each sections* of the test in order to pass. C (I)
8. *Mathematics courses* are not always required in college. (C) I
9. One of the most *popular attraction* in Utah is Zion National Park. C (I)
10. *The* squirrel is a member of the rodent family. (C) I

Explanation

Using *a* and *an* with Singular Count Nouns

Count nouns can generally occur in both singular and plural. It is only possible to use *a* and *an* with singular count nouns, not plural or noncount nouns. It would, therefore, be incorrect to say:

We're having ~~a~~ (some) beautiful *weather* along with ~~a~~ heavy *storms*.

Since *weather* is noncount and *storms* is plural, *a* must be removed.

Some before the noncount noun, *weather,* is optional.

An occurs before words beginning with a vowel sound.

> There are *an* empty box and *an* apple on the table.
> That was *an* honest answer. (the *h* is not pronounced; cf. *a* history lesson, in which the *h* is
> pronounced)   e.g. an hour
>   a horse

Plural Nouns

Normally the plural in English is formed by adding *-s* or *-es*. These endings must generally be
used when expressing plurality.

> A number of plant^s found in Europe originally came from the Americas.
> The box^es contain envelopes.

There are, however, certain nouns whose plural is irregular. These nouns are not followed by *-s*.
Some of these exceptions are the following.

foot	feet
tooth	teeth
person	people
man	men
woman	women
child	children
sheep	sheep
deer	deer
crisis	crises
thesis	theses
phenomenon	phenomena

Adjectives That Accompany Plural Nouns

Adjectives are never pluralized in English even though they accompany a plural noun. Therefore
it is incorrect to add *-s* to the adjective *old* in the following sentence.

> In the closet were one old shoe and two olds shirts.

Likewise, nouns functioning as adjectives are normally not pluralized. Notice that in the following
example, only *factory* occurs in the plural, not *car* or *truck*.

> There are many cars and trucks factories near Detroit.

The same is true of expressions involving time and money, such as

> a four-months semester
> a twenty-million-dollars deal

Some nouns, however, always occur with *-s,* including *news, clothes,* and *species* and nouns that refer to academic disciplines such as *linguistics, statistics,* and *mathematics.* Therefore it is correct to say, *a news program* and *a statistics course.* (see that !)

Each, every, and all

Each and *every* accompany singular nouns, while their counterpart *all* occurs with plural or noncount nouns.

> *Every* ornament that arrived was handmade.
> *Each* (one) of the CDs costs $17.99.
> *All* the fruit and vegetables were destroyed. ¦

The following sentences would, therefore, be incorrect.

> All
> ~~Every~~ ornaments that arrived were handmade.
> All
> ~~Each~~ but three of the beds had mattresses.

singular   noncount -> plural

Another and other

Like *each* and *every,* the adjective *another* only precedes a singular noun. *Another* begins with *an,* which implies singularity.

> Would you like *another* cup of coffee?

Other occurs with noncount and plural count nouns.

> There is *other* information (noncount) about the storm on *other* radio channels (plural count).

The Article the

As discussed above, the article *a* (*an*) occurs before singular count nouns but not before plural or noncount nouns. The article *the,* on the other hand, can occur before both count and noncount nouns, but its function is limited.

we see

The is often used as a reference word. For example, it can refer to an entity that is known to the speaker and possibly the listener.

> "I'm looking for *the* dog."
> "He's outside."

In this example, the speakers probably live together and have a dog. *The* is used because both parties know specifically which dog the first speaker is talking about.

The can also be used to refer to an entity that has already been introduced or mentioned.

> "Hi, Bob, this is José. Can you help me? My car broke down."
> "Where's *the* car now?"

In this example, José makes it clear to Bob which car he is talking about—his own. Therefore, Bob can then use *the* to refer specifically to José's car.

The can also be used to refer to a unique entity.

> "It's a really clear night."
> "Look, there's *the* moon."

In this example, *the* refers to the only moon visible from Earth. Both the speaker and the listener know that *the* is being used as a unique reference. If the speaker had said, "Look there's *a* moon," the listener would have either been confused or amused, since it is impossible to see more than one moon with the naked eye.

Other similar examples of unique references include *the solar system, the sun, the Earth, the continents*. Take the last example, *the continents*. Again there is an assumption that the listeners know which continents the speaker is referring to—the continents on this planet.

Other less tangible examples of unique references include *the housing industry, the military, the stock market, the weather, the south, the wind,* and *the economy*.

The is also used to refer to parts of a whole object.

> This instrument is called a viola. This is *the* bow, and those are *the* strings.
> We live in a nice house. *The* kitchen has a big window facing *the* garden, and *the* living
> room has a stone fireplace.

The commonly occurs before noun phrases containing *of* or *for*.

> "What's your background?"

> "I graduated from *the* University of Michigan and have worked at *the* National Institutes of
> Health and at an organization called *the* Association for Mental Health Studies."

In this example, the second speaker uses *the* three times to refer to three specific organizational entities. Notice that in these cases *the* is part of the noun phrase containing *of* or *for* and may often be considered part of the name of the organization.

The occurs with *of* in many other contexts. Examples include *the establishment of a new court, the introduction of a plan to increase productivity, the future of the world*.

The can also be used to refer to an entire class or category of persons or other animate or inanimate objects. For example, it is possible to talk about *the brain, the tiger, the rose, the musician*.

> *The* musician must be both precise and expressive.
> *The* rose is considered one of the most fragrant flowers.*

*See unit 7 for other uses of *the*.

Practice

Exercise

Study the following sentences. Decide if the italicized portion of the sentence is *correct* (C) or *incorrect* (I). Circle your answer.

1. Modern *messages* systems are becoming more and more complex.   **C** (**I**)
2. There is *an* equipment failure in the language laboratory.   (**C**) **I**

3. Researchers continue to find *another* uses for robots.   C **(I)**
4. Meters are used instead of *feets* in most parts of the world.   C **(I)**
5. *Every* man, woman, and child must wear a seat belt in Canada.   **(C)** I
6. A large group of *tourist* will arrive on the island this summer.   C **(I)**
7. The children's *butterfly* collection was preserved for many years.   **(C)** I
8. I could answer *each* but one exam question.   C **(I)**
9. One of the most popular American *holiday* is Thanksgiving, which is celebrated in November.   C **(I)**
10. A person's *foot size* may change with age.   **(C)** I
11. Many *news story* that deal with TV and film personalities are exaggerated.   C **(I)**
12. *Car* industry has periodic economic swings.   C **(I)**
13. Police officers in England, unlike those in the United States, do not carry *gun*.   C **(I)**
14. *These year's interest rates* have dropped 2 percent, making it possible for more people to buy homes.   C **(I)**
15. In the last 30 years more and more *American woman* have begun to work outside the home because of financial necessity.   C **(I)**
16. During the winter months *fruit and vegetable* are transported from California to other parts of North America.   C **(I)**
17. These days more students are learning about *importance* of environmental costs.   C **(I)**
18. Rabies is *extremely dangerous disease* that is usually fatal to humans.   C **(I)**
19. I bought a garden hose and a wheelbarrow at this store, but *the* garden hose is defective.   **(C)** I
20. Can you help me? There's something wrong with *tire on my wheelbarrow*.   C **(I)**

Final Test

Study the following sentences. Decide if the italicized portion of the sentence is *correct* (C) or *incorrect* (I). Circle your answer.

1. Grandma's wedding dress was found in *the* attic.   **(C)** I
2. Because of the drought, there were *fewer apples* this year than last year.   **(C)** I
3. Only *a small number of* corn will be harvested this year.   C **(I)**
4. The 14-*carat* gold ring was worth over two million dollars.   **(C)** I
5. Some people are planning to vote in today's election, but *many of them* are staying home.   **(C)** I
6. A teacher's equipment usually includes *a few chalks*.   C **(I)**   like coffee, => noncount
7. Besides Bob, there are *another* men who are going to lift the piano.   C **(I)**
8. *Future of train transportation* in the United States and Canada is uncertain.   C **(I)**
9. Did you get *a* invitation to the wedding?   C **(I)**
10. I need *one more wood* to finish the bookcase.   C **(I)**
11. One of the *many use* of bicarbonate of soda is as an odor absorber.   C **(I)**

12. Many educators recommend that the *nine-month school year* be lengthened to eleven months.   (C)   I

13. In the past students needed to know *less mathematics* than today.   (C)   I

14. You must complete *each sections* of the test to pass.   C   (I)

15. *The* dog is considered a man's best friend.   (C)   I

Unit 2

Agreement

— Subject-Verb Agreement —

Circle the best answer.

1. People say that statistics (is) (are) a difficult course for people to understand. *statistics → uncount*
2. Only one of the fifty people surveyed (approve) (approves) of the new tax on food.
3. It is fortunate that the wishes of the community (was) (were) heeded before the new highway was built.
4. The number of people who have children (has) (have) declined.
5. About 75 percent of the students (is) (are) planning to continue with graduate studies.
6. A study of the side effects of megavitamins (is) (are) needed.
7. My daughters' pediatrician (seems) (seem) competent and warm.
8. What you eat and how much you exercise (is) (are) important factors in a weight loss program.
9. Farmers in the midwestern section of the United States raise cattle and (grows) (grow) a variety of crops.
10. They say that many people (is) (are) in a better mood when the sun is shining.

Explanation

When a noun is noncount, it is accompanied by the singular form of the verb.

> The *meat has* a lot of fat.   *statistics*

As mentioned in unit 1, words such as *news* and *mathematics* are noncount nouns, even though they end in *-s*. They would, therefore, take the singular form of the verb.

> The *news* of Kate's marriage *is* surprising. *Here is the news!*

Singular count nouns, such as *door* and *plumber,* take the singular form of the verb. Plural count nouns (*doors* and *plumbers*), including irregular plural nouns, are accompanied by the plural form of the verb.

This *person* always *comes* late. (singular)
These *people* always *come* late. (irregular plural)

The *sheep is* Jo's pet. (singular)
The *sheep were* lined up two by two. (irregular plural)

In order to determine subject-verb agreement, it is important to decide which word (or words) must agree with the verb. In the first sentence, *license* determines the form of the verb. The *license,* not the credit cards, *was lost.* In the second, *doors,* not *building,* determines the form of the verb.

My *license,* rather than my credit cards, *was lost.*
The building's wooden *doors were hand carved.*

In some cases, the noun clause decides the form of the verb.

That the trees lose their leaves is a sign of winter.

Words like *everyone, everybody, no one, nobody, someone, anyone, somebody,* and *each (one)* are singular.

Everyone enjoys the annual folklore festival.

Study the following sentences. What words determine subject-verb agreement? If you are not sure, look at the verb.

1. Large supplies of petroleum *were shipped* from Alaska.
2. A drop in prices *is predicted* for the coming year.
3. The number of books about U.S. universities *totals* fifteen.
4. A number of books about U.S. universities *are* in the library.

5. The majority of these birds *migrate* for the winter.
6. The majority of homework *is* useful.

7. About 50 percent of the crop *was destroyed* by insects.
8. Over 30 percent of the children *have* the flu.

9. The boys' mother *was* present at their graduation.
10. Alicia, along with her brothers, *was* born in Mexico.
11. Her mother and father *were* born in the U.K.

12. One of the most stressful aspects of student life *is* final exams.
13. How the great pyramids of the world were built *is* still a mystery. ✳

In the first three examples, the noun before the prepositional phrase agrees with the verb. In example four, *a number of,* which is similar in meaning to *a lot of,* is followed by a plural noun that determines subject-verb agreement. In the fifth and sixth examples, *birds* (plural, count) and *homework* (noncount), not *majority,* determine the form of the verb. In examples seven and eight, *crop* and *children,* rather than *percent,* agree with the verb. In example nine, the noun *mother,* rather than the possessive noun *boys',* determines the form of the verb. In example ten, *Alicia* is considered the subject and is thus accompanied by the singular form of the verb. In example eleven,

✳ bezieht sich auf das Verb

the two singular nouns connected by *and* require the plural form of the verb. In example twelve, *one,* rather than *aspects,* determines the form of the verb. In example thirteen, the subject of the sentence *how the great pyramids of the world were built* is treated as singular and therefore is followed by *is,* not *are.*

Practice

Exercise 1

Circle the best answer.

1. The women's courage during the flood (was) (were) exceptional.
2. The majority of the TOEFL tests (is) (are) now given by computer.
3. One of the two evening flights to Atlanta (leaves) (leave) before 7:00.
4. Local news (is) (are) on TV every night at 5:30.
5. Small amounts of poison (was) (were) found in the coffee cup.
6. There (was) (were) much discussion about salary raises.
7. Both the table and the chair (looks) (look) uncomfortable.
8. A number of sheep (has) (have) died from a strange illness.
9. That so many houses are being put up for sale (is) (are) indicative of the economic situation.
10. The rock singer, along with his bodyguard, (was) (were) rushed away from the theater.
11. Only one of the fifty states in the United States (is) (are) a group of islands.
12. The boat with 30 men, women, and children (was) (were) rescued by the Coast Guard.
13. A horse's teeth (reveals) (reveal) its age.
14. The capital city of the United States (has) (have) a number of interesting attractions.
15. What the cooks prepared for dinner (was) (were) received with enthusiasm.
16. None of the milk (is) (are) spoiled.
17. Fish (is) (are) dying because of polluted water.
18. The chances of passing the mathematics test (is) (are) three to one.
19. Some bottles of perfume (doesn't) (don't) have labels.
20. Where the Olympic Games will be held (is) (are) determined long in advance.

Exercise 2

Circle the letter of the best answer.

1. "Who has been planning the dance?"

   "Everyone in the club _____."

   a. is
   b. are

2. "How much money did you spend?"

   "As much as there _____."

   a. were
   b. was *(circled)*

3. "We went snorkeling at the beach."

   "Tropical fish _____ such beautiful color patterns."

   a. have *(circled)*
   b. has

4. "Why are you buying all that food?"

   "Because a lot of children _____ to the birthday party."

   a. are coming *(circled)*
   b. is coming

5. "Where is the salad?"

   "Over there. And the bowls of fruit _____ on the table."

   a. is sitting
   b. are sitting *(circled)*

6. The children's bedroom _____ upstairs on the second floor.

   a. is *(circled)*
   b. are

7. "Why did they close the center of the city to automobiles?"

   "Because the number of contaminants in the air _____."

   a. was increasing *(circled)*
   b. were increasing

8. "The shelves are really empty."

   "Yes. Almost all of the food _____ sold."

   a. have been
   b. has been *(circled)*

9. The forest trails _____ any signs for campers.

   a. doesn't have
   b. don't have *(circled)*

10. "Why did you change your major from economics to law?"

    "Because economics _____ as interesting to me as law."

    a. isn't *(circled)*
    b. aren't

— Pronouns and Pronoun Agreement —

Pretest A

Circle the best answer.

1. There was some discussion between my associate and (I) (me) about how to spend the money.
2. Are your children old enough to take care of (theirselves) (themselves)?
3. In order to square a number, multiply the number by (it) (itself).
4. Your reasons for missing class are legitimate, and we'll accept (them) (it).
5. Julia is famous for (his) (her) cooking.
6. Information from a lie detector test is not permissible in court because (it is) (is) not reliable.
7. Every state in the United States makes (their) (its) own laws on matters such as education, marriage and divorce, and capital punishment.
8. (The cactus) (The cactus it) typically requires a small amount of water during the winter months.
9. You take your car, and we'll take (our) (ours).
10. Maria thinks (she) (her) and her sister are coming for a visit in April.

Explanation

In formal English, the object pronouns *me, her, him, us,* and *them* are not used in subject position.

> I
> My brother and ~~me~~ are planning an anniversary party for our parents.

> she
> Louise expects that ~~her~~ and her sister will get scholarships.

Likewise, subject pronouns, such as *I, he, she, we,* and *they,* aren't used as the object of a verb or a preposition.

> me
> Alex made arrangements with Mario and ~~I~~ to go to the boat races.

> her
> Call the dentist and tell ~~she~~ I'll be late.

> me
> Put the potato chips between you and ~~I~~.

In English, a pronoun must agree in gender and number with the noun it refers to.

> *Nancy* has *her* opinion, and *Gary and Ron* have *theirs.*[1]

---

1. Even though it may be difficult to know whether a name in English refers to a man or to a woman, one guideline that works fairly well is that women's names sometimes end in *-a* (*Laura, Susanna, Eliza, Theresa, Paula*) and *-y* or *-ie* (*Wendy, Tammy, Connie, Mary, Nancy*). But men's names and nicknames can also end in *-y* (*Billy, Gary, Bobby*) and even *-ie* (*Eddie*).

As originally written, the following sentences do not have proper agreement and are, therefore, incorrect.

> The cattle were loose so we corralled ~~it~~. *(them)*

> Are you two enjoying ~~yourself~~? *(yourselves)*

In the first example, *cattle* is plural. In the second example, the suffix *-selves,* rather than *-self,* is used to refer to the plural subject, *you two.*

> *Note* The reflexive pronoun for *they* is *themselves* (not *theirselves*) and for *he* is *himself* (not *hisself*).

The following words agree with the singular form of the pronoun (*his, her, its*).

> everyone
> everybody
> anyone
> anybody
> someone
> somebody
> no one
> nobody
> each (person, thing)

> *Everyone* must consider *his* (*her*) options.
> *Each item* has *its* own container.

While it may be considered incorrect in formal written English to use the plural pronoun form *their* in place of *his, her,* or *its, their* is frequently used in conversation, as in *It's raining and no one brought their umbrella* and *Does anyone have their umbrella with them?*

While pronoun agreement occurs in English, pronouns that directly follow a noun phrase in subject position are considered repetitive. Sentences like the following are not correct in formal written English but may be heard in informal spoken English.

> The workers on the farm ~~they~~ have started a cooperative.

A final comment on pronouns concerns the pronoun *it. It* is commonly used as the subject of the verb *to be* (*is, was, has been,* etc.), as in

> Meg thinks a new school will be built, but I don't think *it's* going to happen.

In these cases, *it* is necessary and should not be eliminated.

> First they told me *it* was possible to get a voter registration card, and now they tell me *it* is impossible.

Practice   A

Exercise

Study the following sentences. Decide if the italicized portion of the sentence is *correct* (C) or *incorrect* (I). Circle your answer.

1. The horse is capable of carrying *their* rider quickly for long distances.   C **(I)**
2. Robert Allen, who lived in the town for many years, was known for *his* native flower gardens.   **(C)** I
3. Abraham Lincoln taught *hisself* to read at a young age.   C **(I)**
4. Sandra, along with Jason and me, had *her* teeth checked.   **(C)** I
5. Although scientists have studied the Earth for many centuries, theories about *their* origin are still widely discussed.   C **(I)**
6. Newspapers and magazines *they* have become popular reading material for people with little time to read.   C **(I)**
7. Animals have a variety of ways of protecting *themselves*.   **(C)** I
8. Alan got his paycheck, but Roberta didn't get *hers*.   **(C)** I
9. Each person in the contest must present *themselves* to the judges.   C **(I)**
10. Many people attach sentimental value to their jewelry and are unwilling to part with *it* at any cost.   **(C)** I
11. Do you think *is* necessary to buy a lamp for the study?   C **(I)**
12. The kids are getting *theirselves* ready for bed.   C **(I)**
13. The two of you shouldn't take *yourself* so seriously.   C **(I)**
14. Carol and Paul would like us to have dinner with *they*.   C **(I)**
15. Between you and *I*, this idea isn't going to work.   C **(I)**

Final Test   A

Study the following sentences. Decide if the italicized portion of the sentence is *correct* (C) or *incorrect* (I). Circle your answer.

1. That the committee members cannot agree with each other *has* caused a delay in the decision.   **(C)** I
2. Bad directions on all but one of the tests *have confused* the students.   **(C)** I
3. The suggestion of relaxing the dress code *appeals* to me.   **(C)** I
4. Mr. and Mrs. Wright's talk on jazz *have been* very informative.   C **(I)**
5. There is disagreement between my husband and *me* about what kind of car to purchase.   **(C)** I
6. Every boy is required to bring *their* own helmet to hockey practice.   C **(I)**
7. The basket of oranges, apples, and bananas *was* sent as a birthday present.   **(C)** I
8. There *have* been a report of several flooded streets caused by the rain.   C **(I)**
9. A different approach to the energy crisis *it* involves capturing ocean power.   C **(I)**
10. Lisa Barnes, the new mayor of Youngsville, will give *his* inauguration speech on June 15.   C **(I)**

Review Test

Circle the italicized portion of the sentence that is *incorrect*.

1. The United States, unlike many *another* countries, *receives* a large *number* of immigrants yearly from all over *the* world.

2. A rise in *the* barometric *pressure* *indicate* a change in *the* altitude or weather conditions.

3. Humans lose their baby *tooths* when *they* are young but soon *begin* to grow *another* set.

4. *The* role of *women* in *world of politics* *has* been steadily changing.

5. *The* reduction of nuclear weapons *has* *much* supporters, both liberal and conservative, from all parts of *the* country.

6. *A* small *number* of *plant,* such as the Venus's-flytrap, catch insects in *their* leaves.

7. Some people think *their* cars will be entirely controlled by computer in *the* future, but *others* don't believe *is* possible.

8. *A* small *farmer* who works for *himself* may suffer economically from *a* bad weather.

9. *The* female kangaroo *carries* *its* young in *pocket* commonly called a pouch.

10. Companies routinely *give* a *two-weeks* vacation to employees who *have* completed *their* first year of service.

Unit 3

Verb Tense

Pretest

Circle the best answer.

1. Oh, no! It (is starting) (starts) to rain, and my clothes are on the line.

2. You look confused. (Are you understand) (Do you understand) what I said?

3. Deer (like) (liked) salt and are attracted to blocks of salt people leave in their yards.

4. The Marconi family (has come) (came) to the United States thirty years ago.

5. I'm sorry. I (haven't finished) (haven't finish) my homework.

6. The town (has had) (had had) two big snowstorms before New Year's.

7. My father (is working) (has worked) as a mail carrier for a long time.

8. Last night I came home, cooked dinner, and (watched) (was watching) TV.

9. I thought I would get to the restaurant first, but Jim (had arrived) (has arrived) before me.

10. We (will sold) (will have sold) the rest of the souvenirs by tomorrow.

11. I (had finally finished) (have finally finished) reading this book.

12. The swimmers haven't completed the race (already) (yet).

13. We haven't seen each other (since) (for) four years.

14. Lily and her boyfriend have been dating (since) (for) last year.

15. (Did you) (Had you) looked a long time before you got a job?

16. That man (has giving) (has been giving) money to the hospital for years.

17. Does Randy (has) (have) eight brothers and sisters?

18. We (are knowing) (know) Kentaro better now that we have class with him.

19. I (beginned) (began) the day with a jog around the block.

20. (I seen) (I'd seen) the movie before, but I decided to see it again.

Explanation

The Simple and Progressive Forms of Verbs

Verb tenses in English can occur either in the simple form or the progressive (continuous) form. The progressive is generally used to indicate that the action is ongoing, in progress, incomplete, or temporary. It may also represent a change from a normal routine. The simple form is usually used to indicate a completed action; a recurring event; or a habit, custom, fact, or permanent or semipermanent state. Study the following examples.

> *I'm drinking* coffee today, but I usually *drink* tea. (progressive, simple)
> She *was taking* a shower when the phone *rang.* (progressive, simple)
> Last month I *finished* the chair I *had been making.* Recently *I've been building* a table.
>   (simple, progressive, progressive)

The progressive is formed by putting *be* in the desired tense and adding the present participle (V + *-ing*), e.g., *was* (past) *taking; has been* (present perfect) *building.*

There are several verbs in English, such as *understand, know, like, want, recognize, think, mean, believe,* and *remember,* that always occur or occur far more frequently in the simple form.

> "You seemed confused about the instructions I gave yesterday."
> "Yes, but I *understand* them clearly now."

> "You've only lived in Mayfield a month, haven't you?"
>   I know
> "Yes, but ~~I'm knowing~~ (or *am getting to know*) the town pretty well now."

Simple present tense is commonly used in English along with simple past and present perfect. Past perfect and future perfect are less frequent but are important in expressing certain time relationships.

Simple Present Tense

Simple present tense is often used to state known facts or to make statements the speaker believes to be true.

> Squirrels *build* nests from leaves before giving birth.
> In the movie, the woman *marries* for love.

Present tense is commonly used to discuss a current habit, custom, or repeated activity or to describe a permanent or semipermanent state.

> Susanna *walks* to work every day.
> The train *arrives* from Santa Fe at 5:00.
> Paul *trims* trees for a living.

Simple Past Tense

The speaker uses the past tense to talk about an event or action that happened in the past.

> The bird *flew* away.
> The tree *fell* to the ground.

A chronological series of events that occurred in the past is commonly expressed in the past tense.

> We *ran* inside and *took* off our wet boots. Then we *stood* by the fire to get warm.

Many times the past tense is accompanied by a specific time reference, such as *six months ago, last December, in 1990, when they got married,* etc.

Where is Tom? He was here *five minutes ago.*
The kids dressed up as ghosts *last Halloween.*

Present Perfect

Speakers commonly use present perfect tense in two ways: indefinite past and time leading up to the present.

Indefinite Past

Speakers use present perfect tense (*have/has* + past participle) to talk about an event that occurred or a situation or state that existed at an *unspecified time* in the past.

> *I've seen* that movie.
> The flowers *have died.*
> *Have* you *owned* a house?
> He*'s been* a carpenter and an electrician. Now he's a salesman.

In contrast to the past tense, present perfect cannot be used with a specific time reference such as *three weeks ago.*

> was
> I ~~have been~~ in Mexico seven years ago.

However, the present perfect is often used with less specific time references such as *before, already,* and *ever.*

> I've seen that movie *before.*
> The flowers have *already* died.
> Have you *ever* owned a house?

Time Leading up to the Present

Speakers also use present perfect tense to talk about a state, a situation, or an event that began in the past and may still be going on in the present.

> Ms. Alvarez *has lived* in New Orleans for six years.
> The teacher*'s been* sick since Tuesday.
> Sam *hasn't finished* his dessert yet.

In the first example, Ms. Alvarez moved to New Orleans six years ago and is likely still living there. In the second, the teacher got sick last Tuesday and is still sick. Notice that *'s* is used in place of *has.* In the last example, Sam is still eating his dessert or isn't planning to finish it.

The preposition *for* is used with expressions of duration of time, such as *for six years* or *for a long time.*

> Ms. Alvarez has lived in New Orleans *for six years.*
> The teacher *has been* sick *since Tuesday.*

Since, on the other hand, is used with a specific day, year, event, etc., in the past such as *since Tuesday, since the opening of the store, since I was seventeen.*

> The teacher's been sick *since Tuesday.*

Past Perfect

The past perfect (*had* + past participle) is used to indicate a situation that existed or an event that occurred prior to a time or an event in the past.[1]

> Maria *hadn't spoken* English before last year.
> The baby *hadn't been* asleep for more than five minutes when the phone rang.

In the first sentence, Maria began to speak English last year. Before that point in time she had not spoken English. In the second sentence, shortly after the baby fell asleep, another event occurred—the phone rang.

The past perfect is always used with reference to another, subsequent time or event in the past. The present perfect cannot be substituted for the past perfect.

>   had
> It ~~has~~ gotten dark by the time the electrician came.

Likewise, the past perfect cannot be substituted for the present perfect when it is used to indicate the indefinite past.

> "Can you finish the report before tomorrow?"
>   have
> "I ~~had~~ already finished it."

Future Perfect

The future perfect (*will* + *have* + past participle) is used to talk about an event that will occur or a situation that will exist in the future before another future time or event.

> I *won't have finished* this letter when (before) the mail carrier arrives.
> I'm sorry. By Wednesday, Dr. Barton *will have left* for New York.

In the first example, the speaker plans to finish the letter in the future but not before the mail carrier arrives. In the second example, Dr. Barton will not be here on Wednesday because he is leaving for New York before then.

Notice the similarities between past perfect and future perfect. Both tenses are commonly accompanied by *when, by the time,* and *by,* meaning *before.*

Practice   A

Exercise 1

Circle the letter of the best answer.

1. "Are Sergei and Tom still living in New York?"

    "No. They _____ to Dallas."

    a. are just moved   c. have just moved
    b. had just moved   d. will just move

---

1. Simple past is often used instead of past perfect when it is clear from the context which situation existed or which event occurred first in the past.

2. "Where is the new chair that you bought yesterday?"

   "The color didn't match, so I _____ it to the store."

   a. return   c. returned
   b. had returned   d. did return

3. "You and Carlo seem to be getting along well."

   "Yes. I _____ him better than before."

   a. liking   c. liked
   b. like   d. have liked

4. "How are you feeling?"

   "I've been feeling better since _____."

   a. the doctor has came   c. the doctor had come
   b. the doctor will came   d. the doctor came

5. "Isn't it hard to drive downtown to work?"

   "Yes. That's why I _____ by train."

   a. have been going   c. have been gone
   b. have went   d. will have gone

6. "How long have you been with the company?"

   "I _____ there two years by January."

   a. will work   c. am working
   b. was working   d. will have worked

7. "When are you planning to send the memo to the staff?"

   "I _____ it already."

   a. send   c. have sent
   b. had sent   d. will have sent

8. "Betty told me that you have a cottage on Crystal Lake."

   "Yes. We _____ there since we first moved to Minnesota."

   a. had gone   c. are going
   b. have been going   d. had been going

9. "Can I come by for my check tomorrow?"

   "Yes. By then I _____ time to go to the bank."

   a. will have had   c. will has had
   b. will had   d. have

10. "Where are Ken and Margaret?"

    "They were hungry, so they _____ to the grocery store."

    a. go   c. went
    b. had gone   d. were gone

Exercise 2

Circle the letter of the best answer.

1. "Did you meet Ursula here at the university?"

   "No. We _____ when I started college."

   a. have already met
   b. had already met
   c. had already been meeting
   d. had already meet

2. "I took the TOEFL. It was really hard."

   "_____ a lot before you took it?"

   a. Have you studied
   b. Did you studied
   c. Had you studied
   d. Do you study

3. "Would you like to go to the new play at the Civic Theater?"

   "Thanks, but I _____ it already."

   a. had seen
   b. have been seeing
   c. have seen
   d. did see

4. "What did you do last night?"

   "I watched TV, practiced the violin, and _____ my homework."

   a. had done
   b. do
   c. done
   d. did

5. "Why is Teddy so sad?"

   "Because his bird _____ away."

   a. flown
   b. flew
   c. fly
   d. had flown

6. "Did you go to Hawaii for vacation?"

   "I _____ to go, but I got sick at the last minute."

   a. was planned
   b. had been planning
   c. had planning
   d. have planned

7. I _____ to the same barber since 1985.

   a. am going
   b. have been going
   c. go
   d. had going

8. Did you say that you _____ here only three days ago?

   a. came
   b. have come
   c. had came
   d. come

9. I haven't heard from Maria _____ .

   a. since many months before
   b. for many months
   c. for many months ago
   d. since a long time

10. This book is so long that I _____ .
   a. haven't finished it yet
   b. haven't finished it already
   c. still hadn't finished it
   d. still haven't finished it already

11. Spain _____ at one time a very powerful country.
   a. was
   b. has been
   c. is
   d. was being

12. "Who ate all the cookies?"

   "Mary Ann _____ ."
   a. has
   b. did
   c. ate
   d. had

13. "Is Tony making dinner?"

   "He's just _____ to make it."
   a. begun
   b. begin
   c. began
   d. beginned

14. "You seem to like this restaurant a lot."

   "I _____ here for years."
   a. have been eaten
   b. have been eating
   c. had eaten
   d. am eating

15. "Where was Rupert born?"

   "In Britain, but now he _____ in the United States."
   a. has lived
   b. living
   c. lives
   d. is live

Final Test

Study the following sentences. Decide if the italicized portion of the sentence is *correct* (C) or *incorrect* (I). Circle your answer.

1. A fire protection device *had* a mechanism that reacts to smoke and heat.   C **I**

2. After the Civil War ended, an assassin named John Wilkes Booth *killed* Abraham Lincoln.   **C** I

3. Millions of people *have visit* Disney World in Orlando, Florida, since it opened.   C **I**

4. Gertrude Stein, a well-known American novelist, was born in 1874 and *had died* in 1946.   C **I**

5. Harry S Truman assumed the presidency of the United States after Franklin D. Roosevelt *dies* in office.   C **I**

6. At summer camp last year children swam, rode horses, and *were playing* baseball.   C **I**

7. Students who *did not brought* pencils to the test were not allowed to take it.   **C** (**I**)

8. Television *had been* very popular in the United States since the fifties.   **C** (**I**)

9. Elizabeth I *has reigned* as queen of England from 1558 to 1603.   **C** (**I**)

10. When it touches a cold surface, water vapor *condensed*.   **C** (**I**)

Unit 4

Passive Voice

Circle the letter of the best answer. Some of the answers may require active voice rather than passive voice.

1. The longest fish in the contest was eighteen inches long. It _____ by Linda Rivers.
   a. was catching
   b. caught
   c. was caught
   d. was catched

2. "When does the luncheon take place?"

   "It _____ in the dining room right now."
   a. is serving
   b. serves
   c. is being served
   d. served

3. "Why is Tom in jail?"

   "He _____ of robbery."
   a. has been convicted
   b. has been convicting
   c. has convicted
   d. convicted

4. "A customer named Parker is asking about the dried flowers she ordered."

   "They _____ to her this morning."
   a. were send
   b. have sent
   c. been sent
   d. were sent

5. Home sales _____ in the last six months.
   a. have increased
   b. have been increased
   c. have increasing
   d. increase

Explanation

Using the Passive Voice

In passive voice, the subject of the sentence is not the actor but instead is acted on by someone or something. In other words, the subject is passive, but it can serve as the focus or topic of the sentence.

> The driver *was given* a ticket *by* the police.

In this sentence, the police gave the driver the ticket. Notice that *by* is used to indicate who (or what) is performing the action.

In passive voice, it is not always obvious who (or what) is the actor.

> The story *was told* over and over again.
> Trees *are being planted.*

In the first sentence it is uncertain who told the story. The information is not assumed to be of primary importance. In the second, the speaker has not yet said who or what (the wind, the birds, human intervention) is planting the trees.

Forming Sentences in the Passive Voice

It is relatively uncomplicated to construct a sentence in the passive voice. The following steps are a helpful reminder. Examples for each step are given in parentheses.

1. Choose the passive subject. (*The table*)
2. Choose the tense. Decide whether the verb will be in the simple or progressive form. (past progressive)
3. Put the verb *be* in the tense you choose. (The table *was being*)
4. Add the past participle of the verb you wish to use. (The table was being *stolen*)
5. Using the preposition *by,* add the name of the actor or performer if appropriate. (The table was being stolen *by a gang of juveniles*)
6. Complete the sentence. (The table was being stolen by a gang of juveniles *when the security guard arrived.*)

A sentence in the passive always contains the verb *be.*

> **was**
> Greenfield Village ~~has~~ created by Henry Ford.

In addition, the past participle, not the present participle (V + *-ing*), is always used in passive constructions. Compare the next two sentences.

> The man *was eating* (when a friend came). (active voice)
> The man *was eaten* (by a shark). (passive voice)

It is considered incorrect to use any other form of the verb in place of the past participle.

> The jewelry was remove^d from the safe in the bank.
> **sent**
> The table was ~~sending~~ from California to New York by plane.

Note   Infinitives and gerunds can also occur in the passive voice. (See unit 12.) Gerunds are formed by *being* + past participle, as in *Being asked for advice is sometimes difficult.* Infinitives are formed by *to* + *be* + past participle, as in *It was helpful to be reminded of doctor's appointments.*

Verbs That Do Not Occur in Passive Voice: Voice and Natural Phenomena

Some verbs, such as *fall, die, occur,* and *happen,* do not occur in passive voice. Thus, while it is correct to say, *The tree was blown over by the wind,* it is incorrect to say, *The tree was fallen by the wind.* Likewise, *A strange thing happened yesterday* is correct, but *A strange thing was happened yesterday* is incorrect.

Natural phenomena are often discussed as if there were no intervening force, and thus references to them commonly occur in the active voice, such as *A tree fell, The rocks crumbled, The volcano erupted.* Other events may also be viewed in the same way, and thus active rather than passive voice is used, as in *The economy suffered a downturn, and interest rates dropped.*

Practice

Exercise

Circle the letter of the best answer. Some of the answers may require active voice rather than passive voice.

1. "Where's the old chicken coop?"

   "It _____ by a windstorm last year."

   a. has destroyed   c. was destroyed
   b. is destroyed   d. destroyed

2. "We're still looking for the cat."

   "Hasn't he _____ yet?"

   a. been found   c. found
   b. find   d. being found

3. "Whatever happened to that street juggler?"

   "I don't know. He _____ around here for a long time."

   a. hasn't seen   c. hasn't been seeing
   b. wasn't been seen   d. hasn't been seen

4. "Diana is a wonderful jazz dancer."

   "She _____ since she was four."

   a. has been dancing   c. is dancing
   b. has been danced   d. was danced

5. "What a beautiful suit you're wearing!"

   "Thank you. It _____ for me by a Turkish tailor."

   a. is made   c. made
   b. has made   d. was made

6. "When is the next applicant coming."

   "She _____ to be here at 1:30."

   a. is telling
   b. was told

   c. told
   d. tells

7. "The maintenance people didn't remove the chairs from the ballroom."

   "Don't worry. They _____ them before the dance begins."

   a. will have been moved
   b. will have moved

   c. will moved
   d. moved

8. Gold _____ in California in the nineteenth century.

   a. was discovered
   b. has been discovered

   c. was discover
   d. they discovered

9. Grandma Moses _____ as one of North America's greatest primitive artists.

   a. is thought of
   b. has thought of

   c. has been thinking of
   d. is thinking of

10. All luggage _____ before departure.

    a. will checked
    b. will has checked

    c. will be checked
    d. will been checked

11. Lava flows from the volcano _____.

    a. have been increasing
    b. were increased

    c. have been increase
    d. have been increased

12. Katherine _____ at Robert's house every night this week.

    a. has been eaten.
    b. has eating

    c. is being eaten
    d. has been eating

13. "Where did you get these old dresses?"

    "We _____ them in the old trunk."

    a. were found
    b. find

    c. found
    d. have been found

14. "What happened to the old mail carrier?"

    "She _____ to a new neighborhood to work."

    a. has sent
    b. was sent

    c. has been send
    d. sent

15. A strange event _____ last night.

    a. occurred
    b. has occurred

    c. was occurred
    d. had been occurred

Final Test   A

Study the following sentences. Decide if the italicized portion of the sentence is *correct* (C) or *incorrect* (I). Circle your answer.

1. Changes in the schedule *have been indicate* on the bulletin board.   C (I)

2. The piano concerto *was beautifully performed* by a sixteen year old.   (C) I

3. The University of Michigan, which *was found* in 1817, is located in Ann Arbor, Michigan.   C (I)

4. Mail *is send* daily to all parts of the United States not only by the government but also by private carriers.   C (I)

5. *It recognized* that insulation containing formaldehyde can cause serious health problems for certain people.   C (I)

6. The caves of Altamira, which *were discovered* in northern Spain, contain paintings by early cave dwellers.   (C) I

7. While some people say that a lot of time *is wasting* in shopping for clothes, others feel that it is a relaxing activity.   C (I)

8. Temperatures *were dropped* last night.   C (I)

9. Lung cancer and other illnesses *can be traced* to cigarette smoking.   (C) I

10. The first census *carried out* during Roman times for the purpose of taxation.   C (I)

Review Test A

Circle the italicized portion of the item that is *incorrect*.

1. Varnish *is made* of resins and oil. When it *applied* to wood, it protects *the* wood and *gives* it a glossy surface.

2. The number *of* young adults with hearing *disorders* caused by loud *music* *have increased*.

3. Air *composed* of various *gases* including hydrogen, oxygen, and carbon dioxide. Today it is *polluted* mainly *by* the burning of fossil fuels.

4. Franklin D. Roosevelt *became* president of *the* United States in 1933 and *has reelected* three times before he *died* in 1945.

5. *The* horse *has been* *an* important means of transportation until the twentieth century, when it was gradually *replaced by* the automobile.

6. During the Gold Rush of *the* 1800s, scores of men *traveled* west to California, but the trip *didn't brought* wealth to *many of them*.

7. *It is estimated* that now *much of* a teenager's time is *spend* talking with friends via email.

8. *Farmers* normally plant and *are fertilizing fruit* trees early in *the* spring.

9. *Many* Irish *came* to the United States during *the* potato famine and *had never returned* home.

10. Throughout history, people *have invented* *equipment* to make kitchen *tasks* easier and faster. Some ancient gadgets *is still being used* today.

Unit 5

Modals

A

Circle the letter of the best answer.

1. "Have you seen Marta?"

   "No, but she _____ be at her desk."

   a. may   c. would
   b. ought   d. can

2. "When do you think the newspaper will come?"

   "It _____ to be here any minute now."

   a. must   c. ought
   b. have   d. will

3. "Mom, can I go to Matt's house?"   // !

   "Yes, but you _____ to finish your chores first."   pay attention

   a. must   c. are
   b. will   d. should

4. "Are you going camping this weekend?"

   "Yes, but I have so much work to do that I _____ stay home."

   a. may have   c. should
   b. will   d. have to

5. "Can I borrow twenty dollars?"

   "No. You know I _____ lend you money anymore."

   a. might not   c. won't
   b. shouldn't have   d. not going to

6. "Did you walk home by yourself last night?"

   "Yes, I did. But since it was dark, I guess I _____."

   a. mustn't have   c. mustn't
   b. may not have   d. shouldn't have

7. "Have you ever played Frisbee?"

"Yes. We _____ all the time when I was in college."

   a. would have played   c. used to play

   b. should have played   d. used to do

8. "Did you stay home last night?"

"Yes, but I _____ dancing."

   a. would rather go   c. would go

   b. would rather have gone   d. would rather gone

9. "Did Greg give you the money he owed you?"

"He said he _____ , but he didn't."

   a. will   c. was planning

   b. would   d. would do

10. "I didn't go to class last night because my car broke down."

"You _____ mine. I wasn't using it."

   a. could borrow   c. may have borrowed

   b. could have borrowed   d. may borrow

Explanation

Modals are words such as *can, may, will, would, have to, should, ought to,* and *must* that occur before a verb and that express such meanings as possibility, ability, permission, advice, caution, necessity, preference, insistence, willingness, etc. Modals are generally classified into two groups, according to their form—pure modals and quasi modals.

Pure Modals

Pure modals, such as *can, could, will, would (rather), had better, may, might, must,* and *should,* are followed by the bare infinitive (the infinitive form of the verb without *to*).

> We *should call* Jim to find out about the game. (modal + V)
> I*'d rather go* to New York than to Chicago. (modal + V)

It is incorrect to use the infinitive (*to* + V) after a pure modal.

> People should not ~~to~~ use fuel indiscriminately.

Quasi Modals

Quasi modals, such as *have to, ought to, used to,* and *be to* (*is to, were to,* etc.), are sometimes similar in meaning to pure modals. However, they are followed by the infinitive (*to* + V) rather than the bare infinitive.

> They *have to* close the road for repairs. (modal + *to* + V; essentially the same meaning as *must*)
> You *ought to get* a haircut. (modal + *to* + V; essentially the same meaning as *should*)

They *used to show* movies in the park in the summer. (modal + *to* + V)
We *used to live* in the country when we were growing up. (modal + to + V)
The professor says we*'re to hand in* our paper on Monday. (modal + *to* + V)

Used to expresses habitual or repeated action in the past, as in the third sentence above. It can also be used to describe a state or situation in the past that no longer exists, as in the fourth sentence.

Would is also used to describe a habitual activity in the past, as in the following sentence: *In the summer I would go swimming in the pond with my cousin.*

Be + to does not occur frequently in informal English. It is most commonly used to give an order or instruction or with *there is* to state a plan.

You*'re to let me know* if you're going to be late. (I'm telling you to inform me.)
There*'s to be* a reception after the wedding. (There's going to be a reception. A reception has
been planned.)

With quasi modals, *to* is not dropped in short answers.

"Why are you studying so hard?"
"I *have to*. I have a grammar test tomorrow."   *same as " I must."*

Understanding the Meanings of Some Modals

Modals can sometimes be confusing because they often have more than one meaning. For example, *should* and *ought to* are commonly used to express a sense of obligation.

You *should* (*ought to*) eat regularly.

However, both *should* and *ought to* can also imply expectation without emphasizing a sense of obligation.   *have to (must)*

It's 4:00. The mail *ought to* (*should*) be here any minute.

Here, the speaker knows the mail comes around 4.00 and is expecting it.

In addition, the meaning of some modals is altered or restricted when they are used in the past, negative, or interrogative forms. For example, both *have to* and *must* are being used to state a rule or an order in this sentence.[1]

You *must* (or *have to*) wear a hard hat when you enter this area. (It's required.)

However, in the negative, their meanings change.

You *mustn't* wear a hat in this area. (You are forbidden to or ordered not to wear a hat.)   *have difference conc. determination*
You *don't have to* wear a hat in this area. (It's not necessary or required that you wear a hat.)

Modals can also be confusing because of their somewhat subtle differences in meaning. In the case of *have to* and *should* below, *have to* (and *must*) implies necessity, and *should* implies a

---

1. "You *must* (or *have to*)" may also signal a strong recommendation from the speaker rather than an order, as in "You *must* (*have to*) buy this hat. It looks great on you."

sense of obligation. However, if we say we *have to* do something, we are planning to do it. If we say we *should* do something, it means we feel obligated but we may not do it nonetheless.

> "Are you going to the party?"
> "No. I *have to* do my homework so I can't go."

> "Are you going to the party?"
> "Yes. I *should* stay home and finish my term paper, but I don't want to miss a good party, so I think I'll go."

In the first example, the person will not go. In the second example, the person expresses a feeling of obligation to finish the term paper but decides to go to the party instead.

Modals and Past Time

Modals commonly are used in reference to the past. The context determines whether the past form of the modal should be used.

> "It's starting to rain."
> "I *should have brought* along an umbrella."   *clear*

> "Did you take a vacation this year?"
> "I *could have* but decided to stay home instead."

Both of these examples refer to a time in the past. Notice that the modal is followed by *have* + past participle. It is incorrect to use *has* instead of the bare infinitive *have*.

> "Did Jan come?"   **have**
> "I don't know. She might ~~has~~ come while I was out."   *clear*

As mentioned above, the meaning of a modal may be restricted in the past. For example, "She *may* come" implies either that "she has permission to come" or that "it's possible that she'll come." However, in the example above, "She *may have come while I was out*" implies only possibility, not permission.

The following two sentences also have essentially the same meaning in the present.

> I *must* get some gas for the car. (It's required or necessary.)   *same meaning*
> I *have to* get some gas for the car.

However, in the past it is only possible to say:

> I *had to* get some gas for the car. (It *was* required or necessary.)

Notice that the past of *have to* in this case is *had to*.

Must have, on the other hand, is used in the past to indicate probability or conclusion.

> "I can't find my umbrella."
> "You *must have left* it on the bus."[2]

---

2. It is also correct to say, "You *had to have left* (*had to* + *have* + past participle) it on the bus," especially when the evidence is even more conclusive. There are two past forms for *have to*. This is also true of *can* and *will*.

Practice

Exercise 1

Circle the letter of the best answer.

1. "Why are you so mad?"

   "You _____ me you were coming late to dinner."

   a. should tell   c. should told
   b. should have told   d. should had told

2. "Why didn't you go to yoga class last night?"

   "Because I _____ for my sister."

   a. must have baby-sat   c. must baby-sit
   b. had to baby-sit   d. have to baby-sat

3. "Helen, will you be at the book club tonight?"

   "Yes, but I have so much homework to do that I really _____."

   a. can't   c. mustn't
   b. won't   d. shouldn't

4. "What time do you expect your parents?"

   "They _____ come around 4:00."

   a. are   c. should
   b. ought   d. can

5. "Have you seen Marie?"

   "She wasn't feeling well. _____ home."

   a. She might have gone   c. She have to have gone
   b. Might she go   d. She could go

6. "Has Tony's plane landed?"

   "No, but it _____ here in a few minutes."

   a. may have been   c. have to be
   b. should have been   d. ought to be

7. "Why are you putting on your coat?"   *pay attention !*

   "I _____ go. It's getting late."

   a. had better   c. would
   b. ought   d. have

8. "Do you like to play tennis?"

   "I _____, but now I prefer golf."

   a. used to   c. used to played
   b. used to do   d. used to playing

9. "You're a really fast swimmer."

"When I was in training, I _____ a mile in forty minutes."

a. could swim   c. must swim
b. should swim   d. must have swim

10. When I was young, I _____ my grandparents on their farm.

a. would visit   c. would have visited
b. used to visited   d. used to have visited

Exercise 2

Circle the letter of the best answer.

1. "Do you want to go to Chicago by bus or train?"

"I _____ by train."

a. would rather go   c. will to go
b. would rather to go   d. would rather have gone

2. "Would you like some ice cream and cake?"

"I really _____, but I think I'll have a little."

a. shouldn't   c. mustn't
b. can't   d. won't

3. The weather report says that _____ ten inches of snow tomorrow.

a. maybe there are   c. there may be
b. maybe will have   d. we maybe have

4. "I'm looking for someone to help me get my car out of the snow."

"I _____ help you."

a. can to   c. will
b. should to   d. have to

5. "Do you think it'll snow much longer?"

"I think it _____ end soon."

a. might   c. is going
b. ought   d. have to

6. "_____ to finish his M.A. degree this year?"

"Yes, or they will cut off his scholarship."

a. Does Paulo have   c. Will Paulo
b. Must Paulo   d. Shouldn't Paulo

7. "I had to take a taxi home from the airport."

"I _____ picked you up."

a. could   c. could have
b. might be able to   d. can

8. "How did Mickey get to work?"

   "He _____ on his bike because he left his car with the mechanic."

   a. must come

   b. has to come

   c. had come

   d. must have come

9. "I'm on my way home. Do you need something from the store?"

   "Yes. Would you please _____ some bread and milk?"

   a. to get

   b. getting

   c. get

   d. gets

10. "Do you think the performers will start on time?"

    "I don't know yet. _____."

    a. They might have

    b. They seem

    c. They might

    d. They can

Final Test

Study the following sentences. Decide if the italicized portion of the sentence is *correct* (C) or *incorrect* (I). Circle your answer.

1. The proposal that *must to be* considered today concerns tuition hikes. C **I**

2. Today the mayor *is to be* inaugurated along with members of the city council. **C** I

3. When they arrived at the stadium, the football team *must has been* surprised to discover a crowd of people waiting for them. C **I**

4. A dirt road *used to ran* through the center of town. C **I**

5. Do most high school students have a general idea of the career they *will* choose? **C** I

6. The weather *may have changed* in the near future because of the cold front moving east. C **I**

7. Kate's family convinced her to study nursing although she *would rather gone* to medical school. C **I**

8. When we were young, we *used to go* to camp during summer vacation. **C** I

9. Tourists take a helicopter over the falls even though they *can be seen* from the ground. **C** I

10. The results of the next presidential election *maybe surprise* the nation. C **I**

Unit 6

Adjectives and Adverbs

Pretest A

Circle the best answer.

1. An (honest) (honestly) opinion is not always appreciated.
2. After Peter hit his head, he wasn't thinking (clear) (clearly).
3. It is (certain) (certainly) that classes will be called off because of the storm.
4. Give this letter (direct) (directly) to the mail carrier.
5. I think Tanya sings (relative) (relatively) well.
6. The customs agent made a (thorough) (thoroughly) inspection of the suitcase.
7. The disappearance of the millionaire seems (really strange) (real strangely).
8. Are you discussing a (scientific) (scientifically) proven fact?
9. A (seemingly honest) (seeming honest) man stole my wallet.
10. I am impressed that you speak (so well English) (English so well).

Explanation

Distinguishing Adjectives and Adverbs

Adverbs are often, but not always, distinguishable from adjectives in appearance. Many adverbs end in *-ly,* such as *carefully, seriously,* and *fairly,* but some, such as *very,* do not. On the other hand, only a few adjectives end in *-ly,* such as *friendly, likely, cleanly, lonely,* and *lovely.* In some cases there is no difference between adjective and adverb forms. For example, *fast* is both an adjective and an adverb.

In order to use adjectives and adverbs correctly, it is important to understand their different functions.

Adjectives always describe, modify, or qualify (limit) nouns, noun clauses, pronouns, and gerunds (V + *-ing*).

> A *dangerous* situation was created by the bad roads. (*Dangerous* describes the *situation.*)
> It is *certain* that the theater will be destroyed. (*Certain* qualifies the noun clause *that the theater will be destroyed.*)

It is impossible to use an adverb in place of an adjective in these cases.

> dangerous
> A ~~dangerously~~ situation was created by the bad roads.

> possible
> It is ~~possibly~~ that the theater will be destroyed.

Adverbs, on the other hand, always describe, modify, or qualify verbs, other adverbs, or adjectives.

> Henry drives *fast.* (*Fast* describes how Henry drives [verb].)
> Henry drives *extremely* fast. (*Extremely* describes how fast [adverb] Henry drives. It intensifies *fast.*)
> The bridge is *quite* tall. (*Quite* qualifies how tall [adjective] the bridge is.)

In formal English it is not possible to use an adjective to qualify a verb. However, in conversational English, sometimes the adjective form is used.

> quickly
> We need to get there ~~quick~~. (informal to formal)

> well
> You sing as ~~good~~ as everyone else. (informal to formal)

> *Note*　In the second example, *good* is an adjective and *well* is an adverb. There is also an adjective *well,* but it generally refers to someone's health, as in *I hope you are well.*

Likewise, it is not correct to use an adjective to qualify an adjective or adverb.

> extremely
> Paul is ~~extreme~~ angry about the broken window.

> really
> These letters came ~~real~~ quickly. (informal to formal)

In the second example, notice that *really* is used in formal English. However, in informal speech *real* can be heard.

In English it is common to see an adverb grouped with a present or past participle (such as *moving, built*) in adjective position.

> Here comes a *rapidly moving* train.
> This is a *well-built* house.
> *Evenly divided* portions of food were passed out.
> The children wear *improperly fitted* clothing.
> Drop the egg in *quickly boiling* water.

These expressions can be qualified by another adverb.

> This is a *terribly* well-built house. (Here *terribly* means *extremely* or *very.*)

Become, turn, and Verbs of Perception

The verbs *become* and *turn* are commonly followed by an adjective.

> The apples *turned brown.*
> The friends *became competitive.*

Verbs of perception, such as *taste, feel, seem, look, appear,* and *sound,* also take an adjective complement, not an adverb.

> The meat tastes *bad.* (adjective *bad,* not adverb *badly*)
> The story sounded *strange.* (adjective *strange,* not adverb *strangely*) } *but in other terms possible*

In informal English, however, it is sometimes possible to hear *I feel badly* and *I feel strongly* about the issue. (I have a strong opinion.) But these statements are not considered to be grammatically correct.

Placement of Adverbs

> *Note* In English it is usually not correct to place an adverb between the verb and its object.
>
>   **the test quickly**
> You must take ~~quickly the test~~ in order to finish in time.
> or
> You must quickly take the test in order to finish in time.

Practice

Exercise 1

Circle the best answer.

1. The lion moved (slow) (slowly) through the grass.
2. It is (probable) (probably) that in 100 years gas will be scarce and expensive.
3. Your mother is always so (beautiful) (beautifully) dressed.
4. Herbal tea tastes (strange) (strangely) to people who drink coffee.
5. Don't eat (so quickly the dessert) (the dessert so quickly).
6. Are you (full) (fully) aware of the dangers of diving?
7. My old car seems to be running (good) (well).
8. The DVD player is a (comparative) (comparatively) new invention.
9. A (heavy) (heavily) built man is sitting in the waiting room.
10. This medicine is for (external) (externally) use only.

Exercise 2

Circle the letter of the best answer.

1. "I don't think Jeff looks well."

   "He seems _____."

   a. fairly tired   c. fair tiredly
   b. fair tired   d. fairly tiredly

2. "Which do you prefer—the blue or the white rug?"

   "For your apartment, the blue one is _____."

   a. definite better   c. better definitely
   b. better definite   d. definitely better

3. "Were you pleased with the translation?"

"Yes. The job was _____."

  a. amazing satisfactory

  b. amazingly satisfactory

  c. amazing satisfactorily

  d. satisfactory amazing

4. "What was your impression of the film last night?"

"_____ speaking, I thought it was rather long."

  a. Honest

  b. Honestly

  c. Very

  d. Really

5. "How tall is Dan?"

"He's _____ than you are."

  a. slight tall

  b. slight taller

  c. slightly tall

  d. slightly taller

6. "How does Amy like college?"

"She's a little homesick, but she's doing _____ in her courses."

  a. extreme good

  b. extremely well

  c. extremely good

  d. extreme well

7. "Would you like to move away from the fireplace?"

"No. It's _____ here."

  a. warmly and comfortably

  b. warm and comfortable

  c. warm and comfortably

  d. warmly and comfortable

8. "This perfume is very expensive."

"Yes, but it smells _____."

  a. exceptional good

  b. exceptionally good

  c. exceptionally well

  d. exceptional well

9. "Your daughter seems to be an excellent skier."

"They say she's _____ for her age."

  a. surprisingly competent

  b. surprising competent

  c. competently surprising

  d. surprising competently

10. "I had a hard time taking notes in anthropology today."

"I did, too. The professor speaks _____."

  a. exceeding fast

  b. exceedingly fastly

  c. exceedingly fast

  d. with exceeding fastness

Final Test

Study the following sentences. Decide if the italicized portion of the sentence is *correct* (C) or *incorrect* (I). Circle your answer.

1. A snake's long, muscular body allows it to move *easy* along the ground.   C (I)

2. In the *unlikely* event of a tornado, it is recommended that people quickly move away from the window.   (C) I

3. *Careful controlled* experiments have shown a relationship between cigarette smoking and certain gastrointestinal disorders.   C (I)

4. The state is *deeply committed* to guaranteeing high school education for its citizens.   (C) I

5. A seamstress's job requires her to work *careful and quickly.*   C (I)

6. In an Olympic competition, it is rare that an ice-skater receives a *perfectly* score.   C (I)

7. Thanks to good reflexes, the driver *escaped narrowly* a collision with an oncoming motorcycle.   C (I)

8. Iron, a *hardly* metal once used extensively to make household items, has been gradually replaced by plastic.   C (I)

9. Stories about outlaws such as Billy the Kid are *largely fictional* or exaggerated.   (C) I

10. A *constructed badly* car can cause injury or even death to its passengers.   C (I)

Review Test

Circle the italicized portion of the item that is *incorrect.*

1. People with *foot* problems *can order* *individual* made *shoes* from a podiatrist.

2. *Many* beliefs of *a* culture *maybe* *symbolically* represented in artwork and rituals.

3. Retired factory workers who were *exposed* to *constantly* noise think they *may have* *gradually* suffered hearing loss as a result.

4. Rules state that all restaurant personnel *must arrive promptly* for work and *dress* *proper.*

5. *Most of the* students *failed probably* the test because they *had to* answer all ten questions *correctly.*

6. People who *take* certain kinds of medication prescribed by their doctor *should not to* drive or use *other* types of *machinery.*

7. The employee's *creative* response to the company's marketing problem *could have been* *the* reason for her *quickly* promotion.

8. *The* public library *will* present *soon* a series of videos on *the* lives of well-known artists.

9. In the past, dog owners *would let* their dogs run *freely.* Now owners *are giving* *stiff* fines if their dogs are not on a leash.

10. Kitchen pipes *used to be made* of *metal,* but they are *slowly* *been replaced* with pipes made of plastic.

Unit 7

Comparisons

Pretest

Circle the best answer.

1. Who is (more tall) (taller)—you or your sister?
2. More (than) (that) 80 percent of the students passed the test.
3. Are you (the same age as) (so old as) I am?
4. Joe is (the quieter) (quietest) of the twins.
5. One fast food restaurant isn't much different (to) (from) another.
6. That's the nicest garden I've (never) (ever) seen.
7. Is the black dog (less friendly) (less friendlier) than the white one?
8. The more it snowed, (the colder it got) (it got colder).
9. (Of) (From) all the large cities I've visited, I like New York the best.
10. (Alike) (Like) her father, Emma has dark hair and brown eyes.
11. Plastic is hard to recycle; aluminum, (in contrast) (on the contrary), is easy.
12. Students looking for employment are taking workplace English. University-bound students, (in the other hand) (on the other hand), are taking academic English.

Pay attention !

Explanation

There are a variety of ways to make comparisons in English. Two of the most common forms of comparison are the *comparative* and the *superlative*.

Comparatives

Two entities are often compared by using the comparative form of an adjective or adverb. The comparative is formed with *-er* (e.g., *taller, sleepier, faster*) or *more* or *less* (e.g., *more beautiful, less expensive, more carefully*).

> A Honda is *cheaper* than a BMW but usually *more expensive* than a Chevy.
> Young people walk *faster* on ice than older people, who walk more *cautiously*.

Generally, if an adjective or adverb is only one syllable, the comparative is formed by adding *-er.* Adjectives of three syllables or more and adverbs of two syllables or more are accompanied by *more* or *less.* Above it would be incorrect to say *more cheap* or *expensiver.*

It would also be incorrect to use the two forms at the same time, as in the following example.

> A Honda is ~~more~~ cheaper than a BMW.

In the case of two-syllable adjectives, normally those ending in *-y* change to *-ier* (*cleanly/cleanlier, dirty/dirtier, fruity/fruitier*). Others are preceded by *more* (*more careful, more direct, more rapid*).

Notice that the word *than* is used to connect the two entities that are being compared. Other words, such as *that, then,* and *as,* cannot be used.

> than
> Mei does tasks more thoroughly ~~that~~ (or ~~as, then~~) her co-workers.

There is a common idiomatic expression in English that uses two comparative forms together.

> "I'll come as early as possible."
> "*The sooner the better.*"

> "Al complains a lot!"
> "And *the more* he complains, *the less* people listen."

Notice that *the* is used twice, once before each comparative.

Superlatives

The superlative form is used to compare more than two entities or to refer to an entity that stands out in its class or group. The superlative form of the adjective or adverb takes either *-est* (*shortest, wildest*) or *most/least* (*most handsome, least comfortable*).

> Small towns are *the safest* to live in and large cities *the most dangerous.*
> The BMW drives *the fastest* of the three cars.

In formal English it would be incorrect to use such forms as *the most safe, the dangerousest,* or *the most fastest.*

The preposition *in* is used in superlative constructions when a particular place is referred to.

> Is Tokyo the biggest city *in* the world?

The preposition *of* is used when an entity is being compared to all others in its class.

> August is the hottest *of* all the months.

Notice that the preposition *of* can be inverted if it is directly followed by the noun phrase.

> *Of* all the months (noun phrase), August is the hottest.
> (but not) Of all, August is the hottest month.

Superlatives are often used with the expression *have ever.*

> That's the biggest ship I*'ve ever* seen.

It is incorrect to use *never* in place of *ever* in this case.

> ever
> Martha Briggs has the nicest garden I've ~~never~~ seen.

In formal English, if only two entities are in the class, the comparative form is used. If there are three, then the superlative is used. Notice the following difference.

Of the *two* brothers, Brad is the *quieter.*
Of the *three* sisters, Alicia is the *quietest.*

> *Note*   In spoken conversational English, it is common to hear *Of the two brothers, Brad is the quietest.*

Irregular Forms, *less* and *least*

The following is a list of irregular comparative and superlative forms.

good	better	best
bad	worse	worst
far	farther	farthest
little	less	least

Forms such as *more good* and *worstest* are incorrect.

Less and *least* serve as opposites to *more* (*-er*) and *most* (*-est*).

friendlier cat	less friendly cat
friendliest cat	least friendly cat
more recent job	less recent job
most recent job	least recent job
most carefully (adverb) written	least carefully written

It is not correct to combine these opposites.

             friendly
Mark is less ~~friendlier~~ than his brother.

See unit 1 for such quantity expressions as *fewer resources, more traffic, less time.*

Other Ways of Pointing out Similarities in English

Other ways of making comparisons in English stress similarity. The most common are *the same* (noun) *as* . . . and *as* (adjective) *as.* . . .

Bill is *the same age* (noun) *as* Ana.
Bill is *as old* (adjective) *as* Ana.

In the second example, *so* cannot be used in affirmative sentences as a *substitute* for *as.*

      as
Bill is ~~so~~ old as Ana.

In English, *like* and *alike* have similar meanings but are used differently. *Alike* follows the entities being compared.

Tammy and her sister dress *alike.*

A prepositional phrase using *like* can occur at the beginning or end of a sentence or between the two entities being compared.

> *Like* her sister, Tammy wears jeans all the time.
> Tammy wears jeans all the time, like her sister. (conversational)
> Tammy dresses *like* her sister.

It would be incorrect to interchange *like* and *alike*.

> The Michigan English Language Assessment Battery (MELAB), ~~alike~~ *like* the Test of
> English as a Foreign Language (TOEFL), is taken by foreign students wanting to study
> in U.S. universities.

> *Note* The phrase *looks similar to* has basically the same meaning as *looks like*.

Like is used in English to show similarity, while *different from* is used to show contrast. *Different than* is considered incorrect in formal English.

> The MELAB is somewhat different ~~than~~ *from* the TOEFL.

Comparison and Contrast: Connectors

Especially in writing, certain connectors are used to compare and contrast. These connectors include the following.

Contrast	Comparison
But	Likewise
Whereas	
While	
In (by) contrast	Similarly
On the other hand	
However	

The first three connectors (*but, whereas,* and *while*) connect two clauses in a sentence.

> *Whereas* (*While*) the chemistry lab will be getting more equipment, the biology lab will not
> receive an upgrade this year.
> or
> The chemistry lab will be getting more equipment, *whereas* (*while, but*) the biology lab will
> not receive an upgrade this year.

Notice in the preceding examples that *whereas* and *while* can occur at the beginning of the first clause; *but* cannot.

The other connectors listed above are used to connect (1) two sentences or (2) two independent clauses linked by a semicolon.

> The chemistry lab will be getting more equipment. The biology lab, *on the other hand*
> (*however, in contrast*), will not receive an upgrade this year.
> The chemistry lab will be getting more equipment; *likewise* (*similarly*), the biology lab will
> also receive an upgrade.

The expression *on the other hand* cannot be altered. So all of the following are incorrect.

The biology lab, ~~in other hand~~
~~on other hand~~   Change all these to *on the other hand.*
~~in another hand~~
~~on another hand~~

The connector *on the contrary* is sometimes confused with *in contrast.* The connector *in contrast* is used when making a contrast.

Human brains weigh about 3 pounds.
Elephants, in contrast, have 11-pound brains.

On the contrary, on the other hand, is used to preface a denial of a prior statement.

"Humans have the largest brains in the world."
"On the contrary, elephants do."

Practice A

Exercise 1

Circle the best answer.

1. This is the (beautifulest) (most beautiful) sunset I've ever seen.
2. Ms. Thornton is walking (more slow) (more slowly) because she just had a hip operation.
3. If you are choosing between these two antiques, the older (better) (the better).
4. Does New York City have more immigrants (than) (as) any other city in the United States?
5. There are (a lot of) (a lot more) inexpensive items in this store than in the one across the street.
6. Karen is (as height as) (as tall as) Robert.
7. We have (the same) (as same) opinion about the president as you.
8. The diamonds are so much (alike) (like) that you can't tell them apart.
9. That was the worst movie I've (ever) (never) seen.
10. Dallas is a metropolis; Austin, (in the other hand) (on the other hand), is a university town.
11. Rashid is fast on his feet (while) (however) Barry is strong.
12. The south side of the island is sunny and warm; (whereas) (in contrast), the north side is wet and can be chilly at night.

Exercise 2

Circle the letter of the best answer.

1. "Would you like to comment on Siri's qualifications?"

"_____ the research grant writers, she's the most skilled."

a. In all   c. Of all
b. From all   d. To all

2. "Brad's grades are really bad."

   "Yes, but Tim's are _____."

   a. worse
   b. worst
   c. badder
   d. more worse

3. "Which dress do you think I should buy?"

   "I like the blue one _____ the others."

   a. more as
   b. more than
   c. more
   d. better

4. The reproduction looks _____ the original painting.

   a. exact like
   b. like
   c. similar
   d. alike

5. "Some of the bananas look overripe."

   "I'm sorry. They're _____ we have right now."

   a. the bestest
   b. the better
   c. the best
   d. the most good

6. "I'm surprised that Mike and Jennifer got married."

   "Me too. They're so _____ each other."

   a. different about
   b. different to
   c. different from
   d. different than

7. "This soup is hot!"

   "The _____ better."

   a. hot the
   b. hotter the
   c. hottest
   d. hotter

8. "Bruce and Merle are creative."

   "Yes, but Ben is _____ of the three."

   a. the creativest
   b. creativest
   c. the most creative
   d. the more creative

9. The harder we studied, _____ .

   a. we got more confused
   b. the more confused we got
   c. we got confused
   d. the most confused we got

10. "Have you decided which tree to plant—the dogwood or the redbud?"

    "Of the two, I think the dogwood is _____."

    a. the hardiest
    b. the hardier
    c. hardiest
    d. a hardy one

Final Test

Study the following sentences. Decide if the italicized portion of the sentence is *correct* (C) or *incorrect* (I). Circle your answer.

1. The *most big* of all mammals is the whale.   C (I)
2. The bookshelf is approximately *as wide as* the desk.   (C) I
3. The northern part of the United States receives *much more snow as* the southern part.   C (I)
4. *Of* the three women, Marie is the only engineer.   (C) I
5. Mount McKinley is *less higher* than Mount Everest.   C (I)
6. The larger a baby grows, *smaller* its head becomes in relation to the rest of its body.   C (I)
7. The *most recent* scientific discoveries appear in science periodicals.   (C) I
8. Are cities along the ocean coast *as warmer than* those inland?   C (I)
9. Ice cream has approximately *so many* calories as two glasses of milk.   C (I)
10. Carl Sandburg, *alike* Robert Frost, was a great American poet of the twentieth century.   C (I)

Unit 8

Adjectives Ending in *-ing* and *-ed*

Pretest A

Circle the best answer.

1. Low TOEFL scores are (disappointing) (disappointed) to test takers.
2. (Scary) (Scared) hikers called for help when they lost their way in the woods.
3. *Gelato* is a (delightful) (delighted) dessert from Italy.
4. The town fire department had the (overwhelming) (overwhelmed) task of extinguishing a three-alarm fire.
5. People are (surprising) (surprised) that Saudi Arabia has such a small population in relation to its land size.

Explanation

Forming Adjectives with *-ing* and *-ed*

In English, some adjectives are formed by adding *-ing* or *-ed* to the verb.

	Adjectives	
Verb	*-ing*	*-ed*
excite	exciting	excited

-ing

Adjectives with the suffix *-ing* characterize or describe the entity they refer to.

> Our <u>trip to Boston</u> was *interesting.*
> This year the School of Dance faculty has admitted some *exciting* <u>young dancers.</u>
> <u>Some of the historical details</u> the speaker included were *boring.*

Here, the trip to Boston is described as *interesting,* the dancers are characterized as *exciting,* and some of the historical details are considered *boring.*

The suffix *-ing* is related to *cause.* For example, if something is *boring,* it causes boredom. If it is *pleasing,* it causes pleasure.

-ed

The suffix *-ed,* on the other hand, describes the effect that a person, a place, a situation, an event, etc. has on someone.

> We were *interested* in the history of Boston.
> The School of Dance faculty is *excited* about some new young dancers.
> The listeners were *bored* with the historical details of the speech.

The history of Boston interests us; the young dancers excite the faculty; the historical details bore us.

Compare the following two sentences.

> John is boring.
> John is bored.

In the first sentence, *boring* characterizes John. He bores people. In the second sentence, *bored* is how John feels. Something such as piano practice or a slow football game has affected him and made him bored.

Mistakes Using *-ing* and *-ed*

The following sentences are incorrect because they do not express the meaning the speaker wishes to convey.

> amusing
> The *New Yorker* magazine has some ~~amused~~ cartoons. (The readers are *amused* by the cartoons.)
> surprised
> We were ~~surprising~~ to find arrowheads near the river. (The arrowheads were a *surprising* find.)
> frightening
> Dracula and Frankenstein are ~~frightened~~ film characters. (The audience feels *frightened,* not Dracula or Frankenstein.)
> disappointed
> The staff is ~~disappointing~~ because they didn't receive a raise. (Not receiving the raise is *disappointing.*)

Common Adjectives ending in *-ing* and *-ed*

The following is a partial list of adjectives that end in *-ing* and *-ed.* Notice the exceptions.

-ing	*-ed*	*Other*
amusing	amused	
boring	bored	
charming	charmed	
	delighted	delightful
disappointing	disappointed	
disgusting	disgusted	
exciting	excited	
frightening	frightened	
interesting	interested	
overwhelming	overwhelmed	
pleasing	pleased	
	scared	scary
shocking	shocked	
surprising	surprised	
threatening	threatened	

Practice

Exercise

Circle the letter of the best answer.

1. "Do you think Margaret will take one of your new kittens?"

   "I don't know. She seemed _____ in them, however."

   a. to be interest
   b. interesting
   c. interested
   d. interestingly

2. "I hear you went to the circus yesterday."

   "Yes. It was really _____."

   a. amused
   b. amusing
   c. amusement
   d. amusingly

3. "I'm _____ that Chris couldn't come to the party."

   "She's got a bad cold."

   a. disappointing
   b. disappointment
   c. disappoint
   d. disappointed

4. "How did you like the musical?"

   "I thought it was _____."

   a. delightful
   b. delighting
   c. delight
   d. delighted

5. "We were very _____ to hear that you got the scholarship!"

   "Thank you. It was really a surprise."

   a. pleasing
   b. pleased
   c. pleasingly
   d. please

6. "Professor Adams's class is the best I've ever been to."

   "I think it's _____."

   a. the most boring
   b. the most boredom
   c. the most bored
   d. most bored

7. "Jim's getting married, and he's only twenty."

   "Yes. It's really _____ that he would get married so soon."

   a. surprised
   b. surprisingly
   c. surprising
   d. surprise

8. "This handmade cloth is beautiful."

   "It's _____ to see such quality."

   a. pleasing
   b. to please
   c. pleased
   d. pleasure

9. "How does Monica like her new scooter?"

   "She's _____ with it."

   a. delighted   c. delight
   b. delighting   d. delightful

10. "You look nervous."

    "This thunder makes me _____."

    a. scary   c. scaring
    b. scare   d. scared

Final Test

Study the following sentences. Decide if the italicized portion of the sentence is *correct* (C) or *incorrect* (I). Circle your answer.

1. They are *frightened* statistics about the number of animals that are nearly extinct.   C   I

2. Persons *interested* in enrolling in night courses should contact their local school district.   C   I

3. Charlie Chaplin was well known for the *amusing* characters he portrayed.   C   I

4. During the long, *bored* winters pioneer women took up such activities as sewing and candle making.   C   I

5. Remarks that children make can be shocking and *delighting*.   C   I

Review Test A

Circle the italicized portion of the item that is *incorrect*.

1. The condor, *alike* *other* members of the vulture family, *has* no feathers on *its* head.

2. The canoe trip was *exciting* until we tipped over. Then we were *scary* and *didn't enjoy* *ourselves*.

3. In recent years, Mexico City *has experienced* the *most great* increase in population *of* any major city *in* North America.

4. This year *the* judges *awarded* the blue ribbon for the *bestest* apple pie in *the* county fair to Colleen Murphy.

5. *More as* twenty *million* dollars is *donated* *yearly* to local charities in this area.

6. Even though men are *physically* *stronger than* women, they are *less healthier* and die *younger*.

7. Giraffes, *the tallest* animals *in* the world, measure more or less *as same* height as a *one-story* building.

8. New York City is an *excited* place to visit; *however,* many tourists are *overwhelmed* by *its* size.

9. Some people think animated films are *terribly boring*. *Whereas,* others are *charmed* by them.

10. Academic English prepares students for *demanding* university studies; workplace English, *in the other hand,* is useful for workers who speak English *frequently* on *the* job.

Unit 9

So and Such

Circle the letter of the best answer.

1. "The new soccer coach seems well liked."

   "Yes. He's _____ person."

   a. a such nice
   b. a so nice
   c. such nice
   d. such a nice

2. "I brought you some cookies."

   "Thanks. They taste _____ good."

   a. so
   b. as
   c. such
   d. such a

3. "The local newspaper seems _____ uninformative."

   "There's not much international news."

   a. so
   b. such
   c. so much
   d. such much

4. I'm in _____ trouble because my computer crashed.

   a. such terrible
   b. so terrible a
   c. such a terrible
   d. so terrible

5. "Wendy is really tall for her age."

   "She is so tall _____ her friends make fun of her."

   a. so
   b. as
   c. that
   d. much

Explanation

Comparing *so* and *such*

In English, the adverbs *so* and *such* have similar meanings, but they occur in different grammatical contexts. *Such* is followed by a noun phrase.

Omar is *such* a good tennis player.
Oh, this is *such* strong-smelling soap.
There are *such* tall basketball players on the team.

If *such* occurs before a singular count noun, the indefinite article *a* or *an* follows *such*.

Maya is *such a* polite person. (singular count)

The indefinite article *a* or *an* does not occur with noncount nouns or plurals.

The baby has such ~~a~~ blond hair. (noncount)

So, on the other hand, is followed by an adjective or adverb.

I'm *so* tired from chopping wood.
Jean dances *so* gracefully.

So and *such* convey very similar meanings. They are used for emphasis to increase the force of the message. Compare these two sentences. The essence of both messages is the same.

This is *such* a good milk shake.
This milk shake is *so* good.

However, it is not grammatically correct to interchange them.

This is ~~so~~ *such* a good milk shake.

This milk shake is ~~such~~ *so* good.

So + an adjective can also occur before a singular count noun. However, the article *a* must follow the adjective, as in

I've never met so nice a guy.
I can't believe the teacher gave us so hard a test.

Quantity Expressions

Quantity expressions *so much, so many, so little,* and *so few* are followed by nouns or noun phrases. (See unit 1.)

I have *so much* homework to do.
The store had *so few* customers that it closed.

Such is never used in place of *so* in a quantity expression.

I have ~~such~~ *so* much homework to do.

That Clauses Following *so* and *such*

Many times *so* and *such* are followed by a *that* clause to show result or effect. The word *that* is optional.

I'm *so* tired from chopping wood *that* my legs are wobbly.
Omar is *such* a good tennis player *that* he'll probably win the championship.

Very and *too* cannot be used in place of *so* or *such* when the result clause follows.

so
The student was ~~very~~ tired that he fell asleep in class.

> Note   It is possible, however, for *very* to follow *so* for additional emphasis, as in *The student was so very tired that he fell asleep in class.* *Such* can also be followed by *very*, as in *You have such very talented children.* While this is seldom heard in conversation, it is common to hear *incredibly* or *extremely* instead of *very*, as in *He's so incredibly good looking.*

Practice

Exercise

Circle the letter of the best answer.

1. "What did you do on Sunday?"

   "It was _____ day that I went to the lake."

   a. such nice a   c. so nice

   b. such a nice   d. a very nice

2. "Did you hear the phone ring last night?"

   "I didn't hear anything. I was _____ that I didn't wake up."

   a. very tired   c. so tired

   b. such tired   d. enough tired

3. "Why wasn't the mayor offered a better room in the hotel?"

   "I don't know. It's surprising how _____ person is treated."

   a. so important a   c. a such important

   b. such important   d. so important

4. "How was your trip to Panama?"

   "Wonderful, except that we spent _____ money."

   a. so much   c. many

   b. such much   d. so many

5. "What is your opinion of the Smiths?"

   "They are _____ people."

   a. such an interesting   c. so interesting

   b. so interesting a   d. such interesting

6. "Did you like the band last night?"

   "Yes, _____ I bought their record."

   a. such much   c. very much so that

   b. so much that   d. too much that

7. "That's a beautiful dress Joanna has on."

    "She always wears _____ clothes."

    a. such a stylish

    b. so stylish

    c. such stylish

    d. so much stylish

8. "I hear that Karen Saunders has a lot of money."

    "She's _____ rich that she takes a helicopter to work."

    a. such

    b. too

    c. very

    d. so incredibly

Final Test

Study the following sentences. Decide if the italicized portion of the sentence is *correct* (C) or *incorrect* (I). Circle your answer.

1. Parts of Africa are *so dry that* famine has become an extremely serious problem there. **C** I

2. Manufacturers now produce *such inexpensive computers* that many people can afford to buy one for their home. **C** I

3. *Casablanca* is *a such* popular American film that, even though it was released in the 1940s, it still appears in movie theaters today. C **I**

4. Is it true that Japanese eat *so much* fish that it must be imported? **C** I

5. Aluminum is *such lightweight* that it can be used as paper or foil. C **I**

Unit 10

Word Classification

Circle the best answer.

1. Many people prefer vinegar to commercial window cleaners because it is safe and (economic) (economical).

2. Grace Kelly's (entry) (enter) into the world of acting began with a cigarette commercial.

3. High taxes placed on (importationed) (imported) goods by the British sparked the American Revolution.

4. The cellist Pablo Casals is one of the most famous (musicals) (musicians) of all time.

5. A (delayance) (delay) in production can mean the loss of millions of dollars to a company.

6. Baseball bats made for (professional) (profession) use are finely crafted.

7. The (documental) (documentary) film *Hoop Dreams* is about two young basketball players who aspire to become professionals.

8. In most American cities police can fine apartment dwellers who cause a (disturb) (disturbance).

9. Mystery books sometimes contain the character of an (aristocratic) (aristocratical) elderly woman who likes solving murders.

10. The U.S. Constitution guarantees (equalness) (equality) under the law.

Explanation

Parts of Speech

In English, words are classified into parts of speech such as nouns, verbs, adjectives, and adverbs. The word *function* is classified as both a verb and a noun.

> Few cars made today *function* on electricity. (verb)
> The *function* of the president is spelled out in the U.S. Constitution. (noun)

The adjective *functional* and adverb *functionally* are derivations of *function*.

> A space heater is *functional* in that it heats up only a portion of an area. (adjective)
> Cars can now be *functionally* built to provide space as well as save on gas. (adverb)

As pointed out in unit 6, it is generally incorrect to use an adverb in place of an adjective and vice versa. Likewise, nouns and adjectives in English cannot usually be interchanged. The following sentences illustrate the incorrect use of the noun *jealousy* and the adjective *wealthy*.

> jealous
> In the opera, Carmen is killed by her ~~jealousy~~ lover. (adjective)

> wealth
> Winnings from a lottery ticket have brought people ~~wealthy~~ overnight. (noun)

Nouns, however, can function as adjectives in English, as in *steel manufacturing* or *blackboard erasers*.

It usually is not possible to use a noun in place of a verb, unless, as with *function,* the word is the same for both parts of speech. In the example below, the noun *decoration* cannot be used in place of the verb *decorate.*

> decorated
> The children ~~decorationed~~ the tree with strings of popcorn. (verb)

Similarly, verbs cannot normally be used as nouns.

> breath   *to breathe → verb*
> In the winter it is cold enough here to see one's ~~breathe~~. (noun)

> success
> Picasso's contemporaries were astounded at his ~~succeed~~. (noun)

It is possible to make a list of the parts of speech related to a word. Take *philosophy,* for example.

philosophy (noun) (the discipline)
philosopher (noun) (scholar of philosophy)   *philosophise ?*
philosophize (verb)   =
philosophical (adjective)
philosophically (adverb)

Notice that in addition to the noun *philosophy* there is another noun, *philosopher,* which refers to the person whose discipline is *philosophy*. It is incorrect in English to use the name of the discipline to refer to a person who works in that discipline.

> philosopher
> Aristotle, an ancient ~~philosophy~~, was a student of Plato.

Other examples are *architecture/architect, chemistry/chemist, linguistics/linguist, economy/economist, poetry/poet, science/scientist.*

There are other cases where two nouns may exist in the same word family. Take *vegetation* (noncount) and *vegetable* (count) or *taxation* (noncount) and *tax* (count), for example. These words cannot be interchanged because of their basic difference in meaning. This is also true of some adjectives, such as *economic,* which refers to the economy (*economic indicators, economic health*), and *economical,* which means inexpensive or money saving. A dictionary is helpful in understanding differences in the meanings of these words.

Because there are so many ways to form derivations in English, it is sometimes thought that a word exists in English when it really doesn't.   *e.g. "to beautify"*

> collapse
> The ~~collapsation~~ of the government happened overnight.

There is no word *collapsation* in English. Both the noun and the verb are *collapse.*

Parallel Structure

In sentences where parallel structure occurs, it is important to use the same parts of speech when possible.

> Telephones are *fast, convenient,* and *economical.* (adjectives)
> Some stage actors can *sing, dance,* and *act.* (verbs)

The following are examples where the correct parallel structure was not maintained.

>   **writer**
> Benjamin Franklin was a scientist, statesman, and ~~wrote~~. (nouns)
>
>   **rainy**
> Weather in the tropics is often ~~rain~~, humid, and hot. (adjectives)
>
>   **taste**
> Blind people often develop an acute sense of sound, touch, and ~~tasting~~. (nouns)

Notice in the last example that the noun *taste* is chosen over the gerund *tasting.*

Word Classification Lists

It is helpful to keep word classification lists. Here are two example lists. In the first, see if you can fill in the noun derived from the listed verbs. In the second, write down the nouns for each of the adjectives listed.

List 1—Verbs and Nouns		List 2—Adjectives and Nouns	
Verbs	*Nouns*	*Adjectives*	*Nouns*
award	award	difficult	difficulty
begin	beginning	eager	eagerness
define	definition	easy	ease
delay	delay	familiar	familiarity
equip	equipment	happy	happiness
establish	establishment	humid	humidity
expect	expectation	jealous	jealousy
import	import	long	length
indicate	indication	prevalent	prevalence
invest	investment	responsible	responsibility
isolate	isolation	suitable	suitability
measure	measurement	traditional	tradition
need	need	urgent	urgency
oppose	opposition	warm	warmth
prevent	prevention		
prohibit	prohibition		
purchase	purchase		
recognize	recognition		
reduce	reduction		
request	request		
resign	resignation		
sell	sale		
start	start		
surprise	surprise		
survive	survival		
transform	transformation		

Practice

Exercise

Study the following sentences. Decide if the italicized portion of the sentence is *correct* (C) or *incorrect* (I). Circle your answer.

1. The weather for tomorrow will be chilly, *clearly,* and windy.   C (I)
2. Montezuma was captured by Hernán Cortés when his soldiers *invasioned* Mexico.   C (I)
3. Benjamin Spock was one of the foremost *authorizations* in the United States on child rearing.   C (I)
4. Tonsillectomy patients are now *hospitalized* for the day and then released.   (C) I
5. Before buying a piece of furniture, measure its width, height, and *deepness.*   C (I)
6. Louise Nevelson was an American *sculpture* especially known for her work in wood.   C (I)
7. Psychologists agree that it is important for children to feel acceptance, *secure,* and love from their parents.   C (I)
8. Hurricanes from the Gulf of Mexico have caused considerable damage to *coastal* cities in Texas.   (C) I
9. The injured teenager was a *foolish* for driving 25 miles over the speed limit.   C (I)
10. The *construct* of shopping centers on the edge of a city may mean a loss of business for downtown merchants.   C (I)
11. Employers agree that they are interested in job applicants who are responsible, *confidence,* and hardworking.   C (I)
12. *Well-operationed* factories tend to have strong manager-employee relations.   C (I)
13. A number of schools specialize in theater, *dancing,* music, and art.   C (I)
14. Managers look for *dependableness* when interviewing prospective employees.   C (I)
15. George Washington has been described as being *persistence.*   C (I)

Final Test

Circle the italicized portion of the sentence that is *incorrect.*

1. Passports *issued* to Americans may have travel *restricts* due to *political* *unrest* in certain parts of the world.
2. Food, *clothing,* and shelter are *considered* the *basic* *necessitates.*
3. Unmanned rocket ships sent to outer space can *effectively* *communicate* with *scientifics* on Earth by means of complex *computerized* equipment.
4. Every year football teams *conduct* *extensive* *searchings* for promising new *athletes.*
5. Some Americans think a *national* *committee* should be formed to discuss *alternations* to existing mass transit *systems.*
6. *Favorite* *condiments* used by the average American *cook* are mustard, ketchup, *salty,* and pepper.

7. Couples _celebrate_ their _golden_ _wedding_ anniversary when they have been _marriage_ fifty years.

8. Many _prominent_ _politicians_ have _received_ _threatenings_ on their lives.

9. Going from an _air-condition_ room to a natural _environment_ can cause _respiratory_ _illness_.

10. Sparkling cherry cider, a popular nonalcoholic drink at _celebrations_, is _bubbly_, _lightly_, and _flavorful_.

Review Test

Test 1

Circle the italicized portion of the sentence that is *incorrect*.

1. Ansel Adams is one of the *most skillful nature photographers* the United States has *never* produced.

2. Many *amateur athletics participate* in *marathons*, which are twenty-six miles long.

3. Millions of people make cash *contributes* or work as *volunteers* for their favorite *charities* or nonprofit *institutions*.

4. *Advertisements claim* that contact lenses made of *soft* plastic are *safety*, comfortable, and easy to use.

5. The *simpleness* of a coat *can enhance* its *elegance*.

6. Mother birds *jealously protection* their *young* by attacking animals within close *proximity* to the nest.

Test 2

Circle the letter of the best answer.

1. "These new trains are fantastic!"

   "They're _____."

   a. so quick   c. so quickly
   b. such quickly   d. so much quick

2. "Would you like some coffee?"   noncount !

   "Thanks. _____ hot weather really makes me sleepy."

   a. Such   c. Such a
   b. So   d. A very

3. "The dance was fun."

   "But there were _____ there."

   a. so many peoples   c. so a lot of people
   b. such much people   d. so many people

4. "Main Market is a nice place."   *again: uncount*

   "They have _____ we recommend it to all our friends."

     a. such good food that   c. so good food that

     b. such a good food that   d. such as good food that

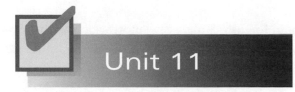

Unit 11

Prepositions

A

Circle the letter of the best answer.

1. "I thought we were buying hamburgers for the barbecue."

   "Some people insisted _____ chicken, too."

   a. on   c. with
   b. to   d. about

2. "What do you think of the new organizational plan?"

   "I'm not opposed _____ it."

   a. to   c. of
   b. with   d. about

3. "I'll buy the cake for José's birthday party."

   "And I'll be responsible _____ the ice cream."

   a. of   c. to
   b. for   d. with

4. "What was your impression _____ the art exhibit?"

   "I liked the work of the artist from Taiwan."

   a. of   c. to
   b. at   d. with

5. "It hasn't rained for three weeks."

   "If this situation continues, farmers will be faced _____ serious crop loss."

   a. to   c. with
   b. about   d. by

Explanation

Prepositions are prevalent in English. Some of the most widely used prepositions are *of, to, in, on, at, by, with, for, from, up,* and *under.* Prepositions often occur in combination with certain nouns, verbs, and adjectives.

> What's your impression *of* the new buildings on State Street?
> Some people insist *on* very hot coffee.
> I'm not opposed *to* the plan.
> Who is responsible *for* the money?

In the first example, the noun *impression* is followed by *of.* In the second example, the verb *insist* is followed by the preposition *on.* In the third and fourth examples, the adjectives *opposed* and *responsible* are followed by *to* and *for,* respectively.

Verbs

Many verbs[1] in English are followed by a preposition. Some common examples are *combine with, depend on,* and *consist of.* In some cases, memorization is the only way to learn these combinations. However, sometimes it is helpful to group verbs with similar meanings. For example, the meanings of *rely* and *depend* are similar, and both are followed by *on.*

> You can *rely* (*depend*) *on* Jason for advice.

Combine and *mix* also share a similar meaning. Both are followed by *with.*

> *Combine* (mix) the eggs *with* the flour.

Other verbs such as *unite, put together, mingle,* and *blend* can be added to this group.

Keep in mind that verbs with similar meanings may not be followed by the same preposition. Take, for instance, *insist on* and *demand.*

> He insisted *on* a clean coffee cup.
> I demanded a clean coffee cup. (no preposition)

Exercise 1

Circle the letter of the best answer. Similar verbs and other words that combine with the same preposition are in parentheses.

1. "Bill and Bob look so much alike."

   "It's hard to distinguish (tell) one twin _____ another."

   a. to

   b. by

   c. for

   d. from

2. "Do you believe _____ flying saucers?"

   "Well, I haven't ever seen one."

   a. with

   b. in

   c. about

   d. of

---

1. This unit does not discuss two-word verbs, such as *put out, call off,* and *give up.*

3. "Where have you been?"

   "I apologize (am sorry) _____ being late, but I missed the bus."

   a. to
   b. by
   c. for
   d. of

4. "Did you go to college?"

   "Yes. I graduated _____ the University of Chicago."

   a. for
   b. by
   c. from
   d. in

5. "Why is the landlord upset?"

   "Because so many people are complaining (groaning, *informal*) _____ the rent increase."

   a. by
   b. for
   c. to
   d. about

6. "What's the short story you wrote about?"

   "I based the main character _____ an old woman I met on the bus."

   a. in
   b. on
   c. from
   d. for

7. "How long does it take to get downtown?"

   "It depends _____ the time of day."

   a. of
   b. at
   c. about
   d. on

8. "Your new tie is interesting."

   "What do you mean (imply) _____ 'interesting'?"

   a. with
   b. by
   c. for
   d. from

   What do you mean by !

9. "Do you drink tea?"

   "Usually I prefer tea _____ coffee."

   a. to
   b. from
   c. for
   d. comparing to

10. "How did you change the class schedule?"

    "We combined (mixed, united, put . . . together) the reading class _____ the writing class."

    a. to
    b. with
    c. from
    d. into

11. "Why do you work so hard?"

    "I dream _____ owning my own home one day."

    a. of   c. for
    b. with   d. on

12. "Who won the race?"

    "First prize was awarded (given, handed, delivered) _____ Jackie Stevens, the fastest girl on the team."

    a. for   c. on
    b. with   d. to

13. "I discovered a hole in the jacket I just bought."

    "Go to the store and insist _____ a new one."

    a. in   c. for
    b. with   d. on

14. "What is a milk shake?"

    "It consists (is made up) _____ ice cream and milk."

    a. of   c. with
    b. on   d. in

15. Many corporations contribute _____ nonprofit entities such as art museums and concert houses.

    a. to   c. on
    b. about   d. for

Exercise 2

Study the following sentences. Decide if the italicized portion of the sentence is *correct* (C) or *incorrect* (I). Circle your answer.

1. I apologize *for* not calling you to let you know that I would be late.   C   I

2. Most students apply *toward* college in the fall of their senior year of high school.   C   **I**

3. Neighbors sometimes object *to* noisy dogs and cats.   C   I

4. Doctors may be hesitant to operate *to* people with heart problems.   C   **I**

5. Parents do not always approve *about* their children's choice of friends.   C   **I**

6. Younger people worry *of* their prospects for finding a good job.   C   **I**

apply to
operate on
approve of
worry about

List of Common Verbs + Prepositions

apologize for
apply to
approve of
base on
believe in
combine with
complain about
consist of
contribute to
depend on
distinguish from
dream of/about
graduate from
insist on
mean by
object to
operate on
prefer to
think of/about
worry about

Adjectives

Prepositions often follow adjectives in English. Some adjectives are derived from verbs and are accompanied by the same preposition as the verb.

> He associates *with* people who are quite different from him.
> He's associated *with* the Ford Motor Company.

However, this is not always the case.

> Ben married his high school sweetheart. (no preposition)
> Ben is married *to* his high school sweetheart.

Adjectives that relate to feelings were discussed in unit 8. Those ending in *-ed* can all be combined with a preposition. (See the list following exercise 4.) Some can be followed by more than one preposition, and many can be followed by the word *by*, which is commonly used in passive constructions.

> I was delighted *at, with, by* the news.

Exercise 3

Circle the letter of the best answer. Similar words that combine with the same preposition are in parentheses.

1. "What's in the jar?"

    "It's filled (*verb* fill) _____ candy."

    a. by

    b. of

    c. in

    d. with

2. "Is Alicia still single?"

"No. She's married (engaged) _____ a veterinarian."

a. with		c. for
b. to		d. of

3. "What's meat loaf?"

"It's a dish composed (made, made up) _____ hamburger, eggs, tomato sauce, and bread crumbs."

a. of		c. to
b. by		d. for

4. "Where does Craig work?"

"I think he's associated (connected, *verb* connect) _____ the Forman Company."

a. with		c. of
b. by		d. to

5. "Why is Julia talking to the school principal?"

"She's worried (anxious, concerned) _____ her son's grades."

a. about		c. at
b. in		d. to

6. "Can you tell me where a hardware store is?"

"I'm sorry. I'm not familiar _____ this city."

a. with		c. about
b. to		d. for

7. "What a charming town!"

"It's famous (well known) _____ its historical homes."

a. for		c. with
b. about		d. by

8. "Can you take penicillin?"

"No. I'm allergic (sensitive, *verb* react) _____ it."

a. with		c. from
b. at		d. to

9. "Is Howard mad at me?"

"I think he's jealous (envious) _____ your promotion."

a. at		c. with
b. for		d. of

10. "Call me if you have trouble getting your car started."

"I will. I'm thankful (grateful) _____ your help."

a. for		c. with
b. about		d. to

11. "Why is Boris planning a trip to the desert?"

"He's interested _____ studying plant life there."

a. with   c. for

b. to   d. in

12. "Let's go home."

"OK. I'm getting tired _____ shopping."

a. with   c. about

b. at   d. of

Exercise 4

Study the following sentences. Decide if the italicized portion of the sentence is *correct* (C) or *incorrect* (I). Circle your answer.

1. Young children are not easily bored *about* repeated activities.   C   I   *(with)*

2. Some parents get angry *about* their children for not helping around the home.   C   I   *(at)*

3. The villagers were surprised *at* the arrival of strangers.   C   I

4. Some people are afraid *at* horror films, while other people love them.   C   I   *(of)*

5. Many people are so fond *about* chocolate that books have been written about chocolate lovers.   C   I   *(of)*

List of Adjectives

afraid of (something, someone)/about (situation)
allergic to
angry (mad) about (a situation)/at, with (someone)
associated with
bored with
composed of
concerned with/about
familiar with
famous for
filled with
fond of
interested in
jealous of
married to
surprised at/about
thankful for
tired of
worried about

(handwritten notes: bored with, bored with, bored with; jealous of, jealous of, jealous of)

Time and Place

Many prepositions are used when discussing time and place. Days, months, years, dates, and times of the day are usually preceded by a preposition.

> *on* Monday
> *in* June
> *on* June 28, 2001
> *at* 4:00
> *in* the morning

These prepositions are not always predictable. Consider the following.

> in the morning
> in the afternoon
> in the evening
> at night   *in the heat of the night*

In English, there is a prepositional phrase *in the night,* but it is generally limited to mean *in the middle of the night* (probably *during* the night when everyone is sleeping).

Some time expressions occur in pairs, such as

> *from* 1900 *to* (*until*) 1920
> *between* 1900 *and* 1920
> *in* or *around* 1920
> *at* or *around* midnight
> *before* (*prior to*) or *after* the Depression
> *from* time *to* time

Prepositions also follow places and place-names.

> on Main Street
> at 120 Main Street
> in Canada
> in Toronto, Canada
> at/in school, home
> at/in the library, gym, building

Prepositions of place can be confusing. For example, in English it is possible to say:

> I'm *on* (*I'm riding*) the bus.
> I'm *in* (*inside*) the bus.
> I'm *in* the car.

I'm *on* the car does not mean *I'm taking the car.* Instead, it means *I'm on the roof* (*or hood*) *of the car.* Another similar example is

> The gold is *in* (*under* or *inside*) the floor.
> The dust is *on* (*on top of*) the floor.

Two prepositions can be used with the word *corner.*

> There's a mouse *in* the corner. (an inside corner in a house or other structure)
> There's a newspaper stand *on* the corner. (outside on a street corner)

I live at the corner of ... ?

As with prepositions of time, prepositions of place can also come in pairs.

> *to* and *from* work
> *in* and *around* the home
> *on* the one hand; *on* the other hand (figuratively)
> *in* and *on* the desk

Exercise 5

Circle the letter of the best answer.

1. "When will you have the wedding cake made?"

   "I expect to be finished _____ Friday."

   a. on

   b. in

   c. at

   d. to

2. "When is Halloween?"

   "It's _____ October."

   a. in

   b. on

   c. at

   d. for

3. "When do people celebrate Valentine's Day?"

   "In the United States it's celebrated _____ February 14."

   a. in

   b. at

   c. on

   d. to

4. "When do you have your lunch break?"

   "Usually _____ noon."

   a. at

   b. in

   c. during for

   d. on

5. "Do you know where Allen's Bakery is?"

   "It's _____ Fourth Street near the post office."

   a. in

   b. on

   c. between

   d. to

6. "What's your address?"

   "I live _____ 1904 Pearl Place."

   a. to

   b. on

   c. in

   d. at

7. "How long is the flight to England?"

   "It takes about six hours _____ New York."

   a. of

   b. at

   c. away

   d. from

8. "When did you study at the University of Arizona?"

   "I was there _____ 1968 and 1991."

   a. from

   b. between

   c. to

   d. at

9. "How did the witness recognize the thief?"

   "He had a scar _____ his face."

   a. in

   b. at

   c. on

   d. to

10. "Have you seen your cousin Hank lately?"

    "He visits _____."

    a. from time in time

    b. of time to time

    c. between time and time

    d. from time to time

11. "Who is Mary Richards?"

    "She worked here _____ your arrival."

    a. prior

    b. prior with

    c. prior to

    d. prior from

12. "When should I make the announcement?"

    "_____ of the meeting."

    a. The beginning

    b. To the beginning

    c. For the beginning

    d. At the beginning

13. "Where should we put the desk?"

    "I'd like it _____ of the study."

    a. in the corner

    b. at the corner

    c. to the corner

    d. the corner

14. "Can you tell me where the bus stop is?"

    "There's one _____ the corner."

    a. in

    b. on

    c. about

    d. for

15. "What did you do in Martinique?"

    "We swam a lot and _____ night we went dancing."

    a. at

    b. in

    c. to the

    d. by the

16. "When do raccoons hunt for food?"

    "They can usually be seen _____ the night."

    a. during

    b. at

    c. to

    d. by

17. "Do you know where the Main Theater is?"

"It's close _____ that gas station down the street."

a. around   c. to

b. from   d. toward

They can usually be seen during the night!

18. "How long have you been living here?"

"_____ about nine years."

a. For   c. From

b. Since   d. To

19. "Where's the car?"

"I parked it several blocks away _____."

a. here   c. to here

b. from here   d. of here

20. "When did you study at the university?"

"From 1991 _____ 1993."

a. and   c. at

b. to   d. in

List of Prepositions of Time and Place

at night

at noon, 1:00

at 714 Main Street

at the beginning of X (cf. *in the beginning, . . .*)

between 1950 and 1960

close to

during (in the middle of) the day, the night, breakfast, the concert

for 9 years (duration)

from time to time

in October

in 1960

in the 1960s

in the twentieth century

in the corner (inside)

on/at the corner (outside)

on Friday

on Main Street

on October 14

prior to

since the last century

Making Lists of Prepositions

Sometimes it is helpful to keep lists of frequently used prepositions in English, such as the list below of nouns + prepositions. Many nouns are followed by *of* in English, but others are not. In this list, verb and adjective forms are included in parentheses. Notice that some do not share the same preposition as the noun.

List of Nouns + Prepositions

approval (approve) of
bias (be biased) toward
change in
complaint (complain) about
discussion about/on (*discuss* is not followed by a preposition)
fondness for (but *fond of*)
insight into
opposition (opposed) to
preference for (prefer X to Y)
relationship (relate) to   he is related to ...

Unit 12

Gerunds and Infinitives

— The Gerund (V + *-ing*) —

Pretest

Circle the best answer.

1. (Learn) (Learning) a foreign language well is a long process.
2. What do you enjoy (doing) (to do) in your free time?
3. Did you hear the governor is thinking (about running) (to run) for president?
4. (Your) (You) living abroad has made you a different person.
5. You can't go to England without (to go) (going) to Buckingham Palace.
6. Would you mind (don't smoke) (not smoking)?
7. When students live in dormitories, they get used to (wash) (washing) their own clothes.
8. The store owner solved the problem (with requesting) (by requesting) the employees' advice.
9. Gina called the police because she was worried about (robbing) (being robbed) by thieves.
10. The team celebrated their (defeat) (defeating) of the strongest opponents in the league.

Explanation

The gerund in English consists of a verb + *-ing* (e.g., *swimming, reading*). The function of the gerund is similar to that of a noun, and, like a noun, a gerund can occur in subject or object position. The following is an example of the gerund in subject position.

> *Talking* to friends is nice, but *being alone* is also enjoyable.

Gerunds also occur in object position after certain verbs, such as *enjoy* and *mind*.

> We enjoy *planting* a garden every spring.
> Would you mind not *smoking* on the bus?

In these cases it is impossible to omit *-ing*.

> Swimming
> ~~Swim~~ in the ocean is a lot of fun.

In order to make the gerund negative, *not* is used.

> I enjoy *not* having to do homework on Friday night.
> *Not* talking while others are talking is a social custom in some cultures.

If a verb is followed by a gerund, the verb can still occur in the progressive. Take, for example, the verb *consider.*

> I am *considering moving* to Texas because of the job opportunities.

This construction may seem strange at first, but it is correct.

Gerund clauses also function as objects of prepositions, especially the prepositions *by* and *for.*

> We collected water *by using* a large tank on the roof. (means)
> The furnace is used *for heating* large spaces. (purpose)

Gerunds also frequently serve as objects of prepositions that follow adjectives, such as *angry about, interested in, thankful for,* etc.

> I'm interested in *working* abroad.
> The Rogers are happy *about having* a baby.

Gerunds occur after the preposition *to,* as in *lead to, look forward to, object to, be committed to,* and *be opposed to.* Here it is important to keep in mind that *to* is not functioning as part of the infinitive (*to* + V) but as a preposition.

> **borrowing**
> I'm opposed to ~~borrow~~ the money.
>
> **eating**
> I object to ~~eat~~ this terrible food.

If *to* can be followed by a noun, it is functioning as a preposition.

> I'm opposed to the *loan.*
> We object to this terrible *food.*

If it cannot, it is functioning as part of the infinitive. For example, it is incorrect to say:

> **eat**
> We decided to ~~food~~ the food.

In the expression *get used to* (get accustomed to) or *be used to, to* is a preposition and therefore can be followed by a gerund.

> I can't *get used to eating* American food. It's so strange.
> Camping is hard if you'*re not used to sleeping* on the ground.

The modal *used* refers to a state or habitual activity in the past and is followed by an infinitive, not a gerund. (See unit 5.)

> We *used to go* to the beach every summer when we were young.

Gerunds are sometimes preceded by a possessive noun (*Melissa's, the students'*) or a possessive pronoun (*my, your,* etc.). This is especially true in formal speech.

> We look forward to *your* coming. (possessive pronoun)
> *Melissa's* getting a pay raise will make her happy. (possessive noun)

It is normally considered incorrect in formal English to use the object noun or pronoun before a gerund in place of a possessive noun or pronoun. However, it may be heard in conversation.

Your
~~You~~ coughing so hard worries me.

> *Note*   It may be considered repetitious to pair a subject pronoun with a possessive pronoun that refers to the same person, as in *Have you considered ~~your~~ taking a vacation?* There are times, however, when it is necessary to make the meaning clear, as in *I enjoy my piano playing but not Sonya's.*

Gerunds, like verbs, can occur in the passive. They are formed by *being* (or *having been*) + past participle.

> Dogs like *being petted.* (passive)
> The mayor's *having been reelected* was no surprise. (passive)

Many gerunds have a noun counterpart, e.g., *explaining/explanation, delaying/delay, interrogating/ interrogation, defeating/defeat.* But some do not, e.g., *swimming* (sport), *doing, sitting.*

There are times when a speaker must use a noun instead of its gerund counterpart. Compare the following two sentences.

> *Explaining* the new budget took two hours.
> The explanation of the new budget took two hours.

Explaining is used in the first example because it is followed by an object, *the new budget.* But before *of* the noun, rather than the gerund, should usually be used, if one exists.

interrogation
The ~~interrogating~~ of the key witness will begin tomorrow.

However, it is correct to say *Interrogating the key witness will be difficult* since *interrogating* is followed by an object, *the key witness.*

The following is a list of verbs, adjectives, and expressions that can be followed by a gerund. The verbs are grouped together by meaning. Sometimes their opposites are included in the same grouping (e.g., *acknowledge/deny*). This list is alphabetized at the end of the unit.

appreciate	begin*	escape
enjoy	start*	evade
like*		avoid
	continue*	resist
favor	keep (on)	can't resist (can't help)
prefer*		delay
	finish	
tolerate	quit	postpone
can't stand (bear)*	stop	put off
detest	give up	defer from
dislike		
resent	spend time	consider
mind (don't mind)	*be:*	contemplate
	busy	suggest**
anticipate	engaged in	try*
look forward to		
miss	acknowledge	think about
	admit (to)	discuss
regret	deny	dream about

talk about	*be:*	have a good (hard, bad)
practice	angry about	time
take turns	bored with	have fun
	committed to	have problems,
end in	happy about	difficulties
result in	interested in	
lead to	jealous of	(*means*)
	limited to	*by* + gerund (Babies can
consist of	opposed to	get attention by
	responsible for	crying.)
get accustomed to	sad about	
get (be) used to	thankful for	(*purpose*)
	tired of	*for* + gerund (Bowls are
insist on	worried about	for eating liquids like
object to		soup.)

*These words can also be followed by the infinitive.
**See unit 18.

Practice

Exercise

Circle the letter of the best answer.

1. I'm worried _____ my final exam in statistics.
   a. about failing   c. with failing
   b. to fail   d. to failing

2. _____ a horse really surprised me.
   a. Mike got   c. Mike's getting
   b. Mike getting   d. Mike gets

3. Many people look forward _____ leaves change color in the fall.
   a. to see   c. with seeing
   b. to seeing   d. to seeing of

4. "May I have a word with you, Adam?"

   "Is this in regard _____ wanting to take vacation time?"
   a. of you   c. to your
   b. to you   d. of your

5. Who is responsible _____ the garbage—the husband or the wife?
   a. to take out   c. for taking out
   b. for take out   d. with taking out

6. I think _____ at the train station will surprise your brother.
   a. your being   c. you being
   b. you are   d. you will be

7. "How do I turn on the TV?"

   "_____ the button at the right."

   a. By push   c. Your pushing
   b. By pushing   d. To push

8. "It's difficult to make money as an artist."

   "Have you considered _____ a course in business skills for artists?"

   a. to take   c. your taking
   b. about taking   d. taking

9. "Why have you decided to quit your job?"

   "I'm tired _____ midnights."

   a. for work   c. of working
   b. to work   d. about working

10. "We were opponents of the political regime in our country."

    "And that led to _____ refugees thirty-five years ago."

    a. us becoming   c. become
    b. our becoming   d. us to become

11. "Did you understand how to use the computerized card catalog?"

    "Not very well. The librarian's _____ was complicated."

    a. explain   c. explanation
    b. explaining   d. explained

12. "How do you like American food?"

    "Well, it's not bad. Now I _____ hamburgers."

    a. used to eat   c. used to eating
    b. am used to eat   d. am used to eating

13. We insisted _____ by the manager.

    a. to be seen   c. on being seen
    b. to see   d. on seeing

14. _____ for contributor of the year must have made you happy.

    a. Your being nominated   c. Your nominating
    b. You nominated   d. You're being nominated

15. "What are you reading?"

    "It's a magazine article _____ your own furniture."

    a. to make   c. about making
    b. about make   d. for make

— The Infinitive (*to* + V) —

Pretest

Circle the best answer.

1. The guide encouraged the tourists (visit) (to visit) the Prado Museum in Madrid.
2. Is it possible (taking) (to take) a train trip across Canada?
3. Now that we've finished painting the house, there's nothing left (to do) (for doing).
4. We advised Angela (don't sell) (not to sell) her antique Cadillac.
5. If you can, I'd like (that you bring) (you to bring) me a newspaper from the store.
6. (To make bread) (For make bread), you usually need flour, salt, and yeast.
7. The superintendent promised to tear down and (rebuild) (rebuilding) the fire-damaged school building.
8. The mechanic needs (to put) (putting) a new muffler on your car.
9. The refrigerator needs (to clean) (cleaning).
10. Do you want (to examine) (to be examined) by the doctor?

Explanation

The infinitive in English consists of *to* + a verb (e.g., *to put, to make*). Like gerunds, infinitives can also function as nouns. And, as with gerunds, it is possible to use an infinitive in the subject position.

> *To find* my apartment isn't easy.

However, it is more common to say:

> It is not easy *to find* my apartment.

or to use a gerund in subject position.

> *Finding* my apartment isn't easy.

This is especially true when the gerund is used alone as the subject, as in *Hiking is fun. To hike is fun* may be considered correct, but it is rarely if ever used.

Infinitives combine with adjectives such as *easy, hard, difficult, good, bad, necessary, possible, impossible, safe, dangerous,* and *nice.*

> It's *difficult to win* the lottery.

In these cases, the subject of the infinitive is preceded by *for.*

> It was impossible *for Ben to walk* on his sprained ankle.
> It's going to be hard *for us to get* to the movies on time.

> *Note* It is necessary to use *of* in the expression *it was nice (kind) of you to carry the wood,* meaning that *you* were nice.

Many verbs in English, e.g., *promise* and *afford,* can take an infinitive as their object.

> Please *promise* me *to be* there on time.
> I can't *afford to take* flying lessons.

Want and *would like* are also commonly followed by an infinitive and not, as sometimes thought, by a *that* clause.

> I want (would like) ~~that you help~~ me with my job application form.
>   **you to help**

Some verbs, such as *like, intend,* and *try,* can be followed by either a gerund or an infinitive. The meaning of the sentence may change somewhat depending on which is used. It is interesting to note that it is possible to say, *I like to swim* and *I like swimming* but it is only possible to say, *I dislike swimming.*

The verb *need* can be followed by a gerund or an infinitive, but it is important to notice the difference in usage.

> I need *to sharpen* the knife. (Infinitive. The speaker is planning to sharpen it.)
> The knife needs *sharpening.* (Gerund. It's a fact that the knife needs to be sharpened, but there is no indication of who might do it. Perhaps it is just a statement of fact.)

The infinitive is often used to explain the *reason* for or the *purpose* of an action. *In order* may precede the infinitive.

> (In order) *to make* better pancakes, add another egg.
> I called (in order) *to ask* you how you are feeling.

In these cases, it would be impossible to use a gerund or to substitute *for* in place of *to.*

> **To make**
> ~~Making~~ better pancakes, add another egg.
> **To**
> ~~For~~ go to Grand Bluffs, take Highway 22.

Infinitives, like verbs and gerunds, can occur in the passive.

> Kerry didn't want *to be operated on.* (passive)
> It is necessary for pets *to be cared for.* (passive)

In formal English, parallel structure is encouraged when using gerunds and infinitives. Even in cases where either a gerund or an infinitive can be used, intermixing the two is discouraged.

> **Jogging**
> ~~To jog~~ on the beach and swimming are two good forms of exercise.
>   **(to) keep**
> Windows are used to let in light and ~~for keeping~~ out cold air.

The following is a list of verbs, adjectives, and expressions that can be followed by the infinitive. The verbs have been grouped together by meaning. This list is alphabetized at the end of the unit.

agree	force	afford
consent	order	
decline	require	It's the place
refuse	tell	It's time
offer		
promise	advise	the first, the second . . .
	warn	the last
choose		
decide	cause	*I'm:*
		determined
attempt	remind	fortunate
endeavor		happy
try	want	lucky
manage		ready
	allow	reluctant
aim	give permission	
arrange	have permission	*It's:*
expect	permit	acceptable
mean (i.e., plan)		polite
plan	claim	satisfying
prepare	pretend	usual
convince	appear	(*reason or purpose*)
get	seem	*in order* + infinitive
persuade		(I called [in order] to
urge	learn	invite you to dinner.)
	teach	
forbid		
	hesitate	
	wait	

Practice

Exercise

Circle the letter of the best answer.

1. I can't afford _____ you any more money.

   a. borrowing   c. to lend
   b. to borrow   d. my lending

2. Our parents encouraged _____ a foreign language.

   a. us learn   c. us learning
   b. us to learn   d. us to learning

3. "Andrea seems like a bright student."

   "She's always the first _____ her work."

   a. to finish   c. to being finished with
   b. finishing   d. to be finish with

4. Please ask the audience _____ during the awards ceremony.

    a. don't applaud

    b. not to applaud

    c. not applauding

    d. don't to applaud

5. "Is your place far from here?"

    "_____ takes about an hour."

    a. For me to get home

    b. To get home for me

    c. Me getting home

    d. Me to get home

6. "What's wrong with this spoon?"

    "It needs _____."

    a. to polish

    b. to be polish

    c. polishing

    d. being polished

7. "Why are you nervous?"

    "I dislike _____ to the doctor."

    a. my going

    b. to go

    c. going

    d. for me to go

8. "Which baseball team do you support?"

    "We'd like _____."

    a. the Tigers win

    b. that the Tigers win

    c. the Tigers will win

    d. the Tigers to win

9. "May I help you?"

    "Yes. I need someone _____ the tire on my car."

    a. change

    b. to change

    c. changing

    d. to be changed

10. "I heard Carla is going to work for an ambassador."

    "Yes. She was lucky _____ such a good job."

    a. to give

    b. about getting

    c. to be given

    d. to be giving

11. Can you get the arbitrator _____ your traffic fine?

    a. lower

    b. lowering

    c. to lower

    d. to lowering

12. "Harry's had a toothache for a week."

    "Yes. We want _____ by a dentist."

    a. him to examine

    b. that he be examine

    c. him to be examined

    d. he is examined

13. "How did you travel cheaply in Poland?"

    "We reduced our expenses by taking the train and _____ in inexpensive restaurants."

    a. eat   c. eating

    b. to eat   d. ate

14. "Your homemade ice cream is so good. What's your secret?"

    "_____ good ice cream, you need to use a lot of cream."

    a. For make   c. Making

    b. To make   d. Make

15. "I'd like to go bowling."

    "Don't forget we've already planned _____ for a walk with the Gibsons."

    a. to go   c. for go

    b. going   d. go

— The Bare Infinitive (V) —

Pretest

Circle the letter of the best answer.

1. "Why are you in a hurry, Raissa?"

   "That traffic jam _____ be late."

   a. made me   c. had me to

   b. caused me   d. forced me

2. "My mother says I can't marry Leo."

   "She should let _____ your own mind."

   a. you make up   c. you to make up

   b. that you make up   d. you making up

3. "I can't open the top of this apple juice."

   "_____ it."

   a. Mark have to do   c. Have Mark do

   b. Make Mark to do   d. Get Mark do

4. I can hear a cat _____ at the window.

   a. scratching   c. to scratch

   b. scratches   d. was scratching

5. "Why do the police want to talk to you?"

   "Because we saw some money _____ from a party store last night."

   a. stealing   c. stole

   b. been stolen   d. stolen

Explanation

The bare infinitive (V), i.e., the base form of the verb, such as *buy* or *go,* can follow the following verbs in English.

> make   have
> let   help

> They *made* us *buy* uniforms for our job.
> *Let* the fish *go.*

It would be considered incorrect to use the infinitive (*to* + V) with any of these verbs except *help.*

> They made us ~~to~~ buy uniforms for our job.
> Let the fish ~~to~~ go.
> We helped the international students (to) learn their way around town.

The verb *have* in English has a similar meaning to *ask to, tell to,* as in

> We *had* the mechanic fix our car. (We asked/told the mechanic to fix our car.)

In the above example, there is an implication that fixing the car is part of the mechanic's job or that she or he is willing to do it.

It is possible to use *have* in the imperative or command form.

> *Have* William open the window. (imperative)

Here, the speaker is telling someone to ask or tell William to open the window.

Have can also be followed by the past participle.

> We had our car *fixed* (likely by the mechanic). (past participle)
> Mark had his bicycle *flown* to France for the race. (past participle)

In these examples, the emphasis is on what was done, rather than on who did it.

The bare infinitive is also found after verbs of perception such as

> see
> watch
> feel
> hear
> listen to
> notice

However, if there is a progressive or repetitive aspect to the sentence, the present participle (V + *-ing*) can be used instead.

> I *hear* the delivery trucks *go* by every day.
> I *heard* the delivery trucks *going* by all morning.
> I *hear* the delivery trucks *going* by now.

These verbs of perception can also be followed by the past participle, either in the simple or the progressive form, indicating a passive construction.

> We *saw* the prizes *given out* (by someone). (past participle)
> We *watched* the movie *being made.* (*be* + *-ing* + past participle)

Practice

Exercise

Circle the letter of the best answer.

1. Have the movers _____ the bed first.
   - a. brought in
   - b. to bring in
   - c. bring in
   - d. bringing in

2. Do you know what _____ the residents of this village evacuate their homes?
   - a. forced
   - b. made
   - c. caused
   - d. convinced

3. "Where are the children?"

   "I saw _____ in the school yard."
   - a. them to play
   - b. them playing
   - c. they playing
   - d. playing them

4. "Look at the kitchen floor! What a mess!"

   "_____ what happened."
   - a. Let me tell you
   - b. Let me to tell you
   - c. Allow me tell you
   - d. Allow me to told you

5. Is it possible _____ you at noon?
   - a. for seeing
   - b. to see
   - c. to be seen
   - d. for see

6. "Your hair looks nice."

   "Thanks. I had it _____."
   - a. cut
   - b. cutted
   - c. to be cut
   - d. cut it

7. We saw our favorite musical _____ on stage in Seattle.
   - a. perform
   - b. performing
   - c. performed
   - d. had performed

8. "Where are the goats?"

   "I had Kim _____ them to the barn."
   - a. take
   - b. to take
   - c. taken
   - d. taking

9. "Do you need someone to water your plants while you're on vacation?"

   "Oh, no, thanks. I'll _____ my daughter to do it."
   - a. let
   - b. get
   - c. have
   - d. make

10. "Ken is sick and can't go to the sales meeting in Tucson."

    "_____ instead."

    a. Has Jessica gone   c. Have Jessica gone
    b. Have Jessica go   d. Has Jessica go

Additional Practice

Exercise 1

Circle the letter of the best answer.

1. "You're late getting home."

   "My supervisor made _____ some photocopying before I left work."

   a. me to do   c. me doing
   b. me do   d. me to doing

2. "How did you get such good tickets to the concert?"

   "We were the first people _____."

   a. to arrive   c. to arriving
   b. to be arriving   d. arrive

3. I'm looking forward _____ to the Shakespeare festival.

   a. you go   c. to going
   b. going   d. to go

4. "Why don't you watch TV much?"

   "I'm tired _____ all these commercials."

   a. about watching   c. with watching
   b. of watching   d. to watch

5. Some teenagers are not used to _____ early on a Saturday morning.

   a. be awakened   c. awaken
   b. being awakened   d. awake

6. "Can I help you?"

   "Yes. Is it possible _____ a telephone card here?"

   a. my purchasing   c. for me to purchase
   b. purchase   d. for purchase

7. "What's wrong with the light?"

   "The bulb needs _____."

   a. to change   c. changing it
   b. change   d. to be changed

8. "The corporate finances seem to be in trouble."

   "I hope _____ as a financial consultant will help in the situation."

   a. George comes   c. George's coming
   b. George to come   d. George coming

9. "Do you like living alone?"

   "Yes, but I'm not used _____ every night."

   a. to cook   c. cooking
   b. to cooking   d. to have cooked

10. "It's getting cold outside."

    "I had Karen _____ the window."

    a. closed   c. to close
    b. closing   d. close

11. "Is Matt still developing photographs?"

    "No. He stopped _____ a nap."

    a. take   c. to take
    b. taking   d. for taking

12. "My sister said you telephoned last night."

    "Yes. I called _____ if you'd like to go out for Chinese food."

    a. to see   c. for see
    b. for seeing   d. because to see

13. "You don't go to the ocean often?"

    "I dislike _____ in saltwater."

    a. swimming   c. for me to swim
    b. to swim   d. my swimming

14. "I'm thinking about taking some art classes at the museum."

    "The last day of _____ is tomorrow."

    a. registering   c. register
    b. registration   d. be registering

15. "What are these rags for?"

    "I use them for _____ the furniture."

    a. dust   c. dusting
    b. to dust   d. dusted

Exercise 2

Circle the letter of the best answer.

1. "Why did Joy call?"

   "She wants _____ her load some boxes into her car."

   a. that we help   c. us helping
   b. us help   d. us to help

2. "How did the prisoner escape?"

   "By climbing a fence and _____ someone's car."

   a. steal   c. from stealing
   b. to steal   d. stealing

3. "What are you looking at?"

   "We just saw _____ by a golf ball."

   a. someone hitted   c. someone being hit
   b. hit someone   d. someone being hitting

4. "What is this letter about?"

   "It's in regard _____ at the lawyer's club next week."

   a. to you speak   c. of your speaking
   b. to your speaking   d. to you speaking

5. "Why are you getting new glasses?"

   "Because it's difficult _____ the small print in the newspaper."

   a. to read for me   c. I read
   b. my reading   d. for me to read

6. "This cabinet is beautiful. Did you make it yourself?"

   "No. I had _____."

   a. it built   c. to build it
   b. built it   d. it build

7. Don't walk home in the rain. We insist _____ in our car.

   a. you to come   c. on you coming
   b. on your coming   d. for you to come

8. "Gas is getting more and more expensive."

   "Yes. I'm thinking _____ my bike to work."

   a. to ride   c. of ride
   b. to riding   d. about riding

9. "You take a lot of nice photographs."

   "Thanks. I'm considering _____ a professional photographer."

   a. becoming   c. to become
   b. about become   d. about becoming

10. Rachel's semester in London led to _____ an Englishman.

   a. her marry   c. her being married
   b. her to marry   d. her marrying

Final Test

Study the following sentences. Decide if the italicized portion of the sentence is *correct* (C) or *incorrect* (I). Circle your answer.

1. Most vacationers enjoy playing sports or *relax*.   **C   I**

2. Heart patients are warned *don't eat* foods high in cholesterol because of the potential danger.   **C   I**

3. Many people enjoy Japanese food once they *get used to eating* raw fish.   **C   I**

4. In general, Americans think *to retire* at age sixty-five, if they can afford it.   **C   I**

5. Chefs in established restaurants concern themselves with *the preparing* of gourmet dishes.   **C   I**

6. Some northerners traditionally make arrangements *for go* south during the winter months.   **C   I**

7. Scientific journals may be difficult for nonscientists *to read*.   **C   I**

8. Some cars now have a mechanism *to informing* drivers of their location.   **C   I**

9. Ergonomic consultants are known for their skill *in furnishing* homes and office buildings.   **C   I**

10. Police attempt to stop teenagers *from driving* too fast.   **C   I**

This is an alphabetized list of verbs, adjectives, and expressions that can be followed by a gerund.

acknowledge	consist of	escape
admit (to)	contemplate	evade
angry about	continue*	favor
anticipate	defer from	finish
appreciate	delay	get (be) used to
avoid	deny	get accustomed to
begin*	detest	give up
bored with	discuss	happy about
busy	dislike	have a good (hard, bad)
can't resist (can't help)	dream about	time
can't stand (bear)*	end in	have fun
committed to	engaged in	have problems,
consider	enjoy	difficulties

insist on	object to	responsible for
interested in	opposed to	result in
jealous of	postpone	sad about
keep (on)	practice	spend time
lead to	prefer*	start*
like*		stop
limited to	(*purpose*)	suggest**
look forward to	*for* + gerund (Bowls are	take turns
	for eating liquids like	talk about
(*means*)	soup.)	thankful for
by + gerund (Babies		think about
can get attention by	put off	tired of
crying.)	quit	tolerate
	regret	try*
mind (don't mind)	resent	worried about
miss	resist	

*These words can also be followed by the infinitive.
**See unit 18.

This is an alphabetized list of verbs, adjectives, and expressions that can be followed by an infinitive.

acceptable	fortunate	ready
advise	get	
afford	give permission	(*reason or purpose*)
agree	happy	*in order* + infinitive
aim	have permission	(I called [in order] to
allow	hesitate	invite you to dinner.)
appear	invite	
arrange	It's the place	refuse
attempt	It's time	reluctant
cause	learn	remind
choose	lucky	require
claim	manage	satisfying
consent	mean (i.e., *plan*)	seem
convince	offer	teach
decide	order	tell
decline	permit	the first, the second . . .
determined	persuade	the last
encourage	plan	try
endeavor	polite	urge
expect	prepare	usual
forbid	pretend	wait
force	promise	want
		warn

Review Test

Test 1

Circle the italicized portion of the sentence that is *incorrect*.

1. *It* is important *to have* the proper cutting tools *for construct* plastic furniture *correctly*.

2. A thorough *investigation of* the guidebook led *to* *our* *identify* the bird as a purple martin.

3. Even though Americans usually do not need a visa *to travel* in Europe, they *are prevented* *to enter* a country if they do not have *a* valid passport.

4. Photocopiers *are used* to *reduce* the print size of a page as well as *making* *copies* of a written text.

5. Police *attempt to* prevent motorists *from* *speed* *on* highways.

Test 2

Circle the letter of the best answer.

1. "Tom made a lot of long distance calls last month."

   "And now his roommates are faced _____ a huge bill."

   a. to   c. toward
   b. with   d. at

2. "What kind of job is Adrienne looking for?"

   "She's interested _____ a career in TV."

   a. in   c. to
   b. on   d. for

3. "How much does a gold ring cost?"

   "It depends _____ the quality of the gold."

   a. to   c. of
   b. on   d. about

4. "I'm building a table."

   "Can I persuade _____ me how to make one?"

   a. you to teach

   b. that you teach

   c. your teaching

   d. for you to teach

5. "When did you get married?"

   "_____ 1999."

   a. On

   b. In

   c. At

   d. To

That Clauses and Interrogative Clauses

Pretest

Circle the best answer.

1. Marcy White, who has been the bank manager for thirty years, announced (what) (that) she will retire in July.
2. (The fire destroyed) (That the fire destroyed) so many homes is a tragedy.
3. Do you remember when (are the guests) (the guests are) supposed to arrive?
4. (How many eggs a hen lays) (How many eggs does a hen lay) is an important factor in chicken farming.
5. It's not certain (whether or not) (if or not) the fog will lift before we set out on vacation.

Explanation

That Clauses

In English it is common to find a statement functioning as the subject or object of a sentence. These embedded clauses are referred to as *that* clauses. The following are examples of *that* clauses functioning as direct objects.

> Your teacher thinks (*that*) *you will pass the test.*
> Do you remember (*that*) *tomorrow is Mom's birthday?*

Both *that you will pass the test* and *that tomorrow is Mom's birthday* function as direct objects. The word *that* in these sentences is optional.

That clauses can also serve as subjects of a sentence.

> *That you're getting married* is a surprise!
> *That it's snowing* prevents the truckers from transporting the goods.

Both *that you're getting married* and *that it's snowing* function as subjects. The word *that* is not optional in the subject clause.

Interrogative Clauses

Like statements, questions can also serve as the subject or object of a sentence. These embedded questions are generally referred to as interrogative clauses.

Maria doesn't know *who is coming to the party.*
I wonder *what caused Tom to be late.*

Who is coming to the party and *what caused Tom to be late* function as direct objects in the above sentences.

Like *that* clauses, interrogative clauses can function as the subject of a sentence.

How much money a person makes is normally not a question Americans ask.
Where the exam will be is not yet known.

Interrogative clauses do not have the same structure as questions. They generally do not contain subject-modal or *be* inversion.

Do you know when ~~will the garbage truck~~ arrive? **the garbage truck will**

I wonder what ~~are we~~ supposed to do with the recycling. **we are**

Nor do the auxiliaries *do, does,* and *did* generally occur in interrogative clauses. Notice the subject + V construction in this sentence.

How many languages ~~does Jon speak~~ amazes me. **Jon speaks**

Interrogative "yes-no" clauses (yes-no questions) can also function as subjects and objects.

Ask Jill *if (whether) she is applying for a job.* (object)
Whether (or not) the dog bites depends on who comes to the house. (subject)

In object clauses *whether* and *if* cannot be used together.

Please tell me ~~whether if~~ it's possible to get a social security number. **whether (or if)**

It is also incorrect to use the expression *if or not* instead of *whether or not.*

Do you know ~~if~~ or not the post office is open? **whether**

It is possible, however, to use *if* and *or not* in the object clause as long as they are separated. (*Do you know if the post office is open or not?*) *Whether* can also be used this way.

If and *whether (or not)* can both be used in object clauses. However, *whether* but not *if* is used in the subject clause.

~~If~~ or not you decide to take the job is not my concern. **Whether**

The following is a list of some common verbs after which *that* and interrogative clauses commonly occur.

believe	find out	remember
think	ask	forget
know	say	see
understand	tell	
	explain	
	teach	

Practice

Exercise

Circle the letter of the best answer.

1. _____ becoming extinct is of great concern to zoologists.

   a. That giant pandas are   c. Giant pandas are
   b. Are giant pandas   d. That giant pandas

2. "I'm looking for the mail. Do you know _____?"
   "Probably after 4:00."

   a. when it will arrive   c. when does it arrive
   b. when it does arrive   d. when will it arrive

3. "Could you help me for a while?"
   "Sure. Tell me what _____ me to do."

   a. you want   c. do you want
   b. want   d. you do want

4. _____ is a question astronomers have posed.

   a. How many moons does Pluto have   c. Pluto has how many moons
   b. How many moons Pluto has   d. How many moons has Pluto

5. Because of the rain, people are calling to ask _____ take place.

   a. whether the parade will   c. the parade will
   b. if or not the parade will   d. will the parade

6. Scientists have long attempted to find out _____ there is life on other planets.

   a. if or not   c. whether or not
   b. whether if   d. whether not

7. "Look at the new DVD player Carrie bought."
   "I wonder how _____ such an expensive gadget."

   a. could she afford   c. could she afforded
   b. she could afford   d. she could to afford

8. "I haven't seen you for a long time."
   "Yes. I'm sorry, but I've forgotten _____."

   a. that your name is   c. who your name is
   b. what is your name   d. what your name is

9. _____ in large quantities is not necessarily an indication of its quality.

   a. A product is sold   c. That a product is sold
   b. This is product sold   d. A product sells

10. "Can you ask for information in public records?"

    "Yes, but I don't know _____."

    a. whom I should speak to   c. whom should I speak to
    b. whom I should speak   d. who should I speak to

11. "The postal strike started today."

    "I wonder _____ something to prevent it."

    a. why the government didn't do   c. why the government didn't
    b. why didn't the government do   d. why the government do

12. "Craig should get his hair cut."

    "I don't know _____."

    a. why he doesn't   c. why he does
    b. why doesn't he   d. why does he

13. "Are you planning to go to college?"

    "_____ I go depends on my financial situation."

    a. If or not   c. Whether if
    b. Whether or not   d. If

14. "Why did you see the professor after class?"

    "I didn't understand _____ during the lecture."

    a. what she was talking about   c. that she was talking about
    b. what was she talking about   d. about what was she talking

15. "Do you know Don Kline?"

    "I remember the name, but I can't remember _____."

    a. what does he look like   c. what he does look like
    b. what he looks like   d. like what he looks

Final Test

Study the following sentences. Decide if the italicized portion of the sentence is *correct* (C) or *incorrect* (I). Circle your answer.

1. *That* an epidemic of measles has broken out recently is of concern to health officials.   **C   I**

2. Scientists are interested in finding out *if or not* the Earth's temperature is beginning to rise.   **C   I**

3. Archaeologists wonder *how the Aztecs built* enormous stone structures without the use of the wheel.   **C   I**

4. The length of the trip will depend on *how good the roads are.*   **C   I**

5. Your choice of restaurant depends on *what do you like* to eat.   **C   I**

Unit 14

Adjective (Relative) Clauses

Circle the letter of the best answer.

1. Aymara is an Indian language _____ approximately one million people in Bolivia and Peru.

   a. that is spoken by   c. is spoken by
   b. that speak   d. it is spoken by

2. Many North American universities _____ by private donations.

   a. are supported   c. which are supported
   b. that are supported   d. support

3. Frida Kahlo was a great artist _____ life was marred by ill health.

   a. that her   c. her
   b. in which her   d. whose

4. Lake Superior, _____, borders on the United States and Canada.

   a. the largest lake that in the world is   c. that is the largest lake in the world
   b. is the largest lake in the world   d. which is the largest lake in the world

5. The Taj Mahal, _____ by Shah Jahan for his wife, is thought to be one of the great architectural wonders of the world.

   a. being built   c. built
   b. was built   d. been built

6. The Tomb of the Unknown Soldier, _____ to unidentified soldiers killed in battle, is located in Arlington, Virginia.

   a. which a monument   c. is a monument
   b. a monument   d. a monument being

Explanation

Adjective or relative clauses function like adjectives. They provide information about nouns or noun phrases by describing or quantifying them. However, since they are embedded sentences, they are usually longer than adjectives and thus often provide more or different types of information than adjectives. They usually follow the noun they qualify rather than coming before it. The following are typical examples of adjective clauses.

> Families *who (that) have children in college* may have greater financial burdens.
> I am looking for a letter *that (which) was on the desk.*

In some languages, it might be possible to convert the adjective clause into an adjective, but in English it happens infrequently. It would be incorrect to say

> ~~Children in college~~ families may have greater financial burdens.
> I am looking for the ~~on the desk~~ letter.

Restricted and Unrestricted Adjective Clauses

Restricted Clauses

There are two types of adjective clauses—restricted and unrestricted. Restricted adjective clauses contain information that necessarily limits or specifies the noun they refer to. The two sentences below are restricted adjective clauses.

> Families *who (that) have children in college* may have greater financial burdens.
> I'm looking for the letter *that (which) was on the desk.*

In the first sentence, the families who have greater financial burdens are limited to include only those with children in college. In the second sentence, the letter that the person is looking for is specifically the one that used to be on the desk.

Notice that after people or other animate nouns, *who* or *that* is used. After inanimate objects *that* or *which* is used.

Unrestricted Clauses

Unrestricted adjective clauses, instead of limiting the noun they modify, provide additional information about it. The clause is not necessary to identify the noun that the speaker is referring to.

> These fresh fish, which come from Lake Huron, are being tested for mercury.

In the preceding sentence, *which come from Lake Huron* is not essential for identifying which fish the speaker is talking about. Compare it to the restricted relative clause in the following sentence, which limits the type of fish.

> *Fish that have a high degree of mercury* may be dangerous to children.

Commas are used to separate unrestricted adjective clauses from the noun they refer to. This is not the case with restricted clauses. Also, *who* and *which* follow the noun but *that* does not. It would be incorrect to say:

> which
> Those fresh fish, ~~that~~ come from Lake Huron, are being tested for mercury.
> who
> Albert Einstein, ~~that~~ won the Nobel Prize in 1921, emigrated to the U.S. from Germany.

In formal English, it is also important to avoid forming a run-on sentence by substituting the relative pronoun for another subject pronoun such as *it*.

which
Steven Spielberg's film, *E.T.*, ~~it~~ was a giant moneymaker, was re-released in 2002.

Whose

Whose can be found in both restricted and unrestricted adjective clauses. It functions as a possessive pronoun and is always followed by a noun.[1]

> People *whose names* begin with A to M should wait in the first line.
> The Great Lakes, *whose dunes* belong on the list of natural wonders of North America, receive thousands of tourists each year.

In the first sentence, *whose* means people's, and in the second sentence *whose* means the Great Lakes'.

Preposition + **which, whom***

Both types of adjective clauses can also be followed by a preposition + *which* or *whom* (*in which, on which, by (means) of which, under which, from whom, to whom, after whom, for whom,* etc.).

> This is the house *in which* I was born.
> This is the date *on which* the medicine expires.[2]
> The name of the man *from whom* the roses were sent is still a mystery.

Sometimes it is difficult to know which preposition to use. For example, *by which* and *with which* are sometimes confused.

> A thermometer is an instrument *with which* the temperature is measured.
> They had recently purchased the ladder *by which* they escaped the fire.

With is used in the first sentence because it typically precedes an instrument or a device (*measure with a thermometer, play with a ball, cook with pots and pans*). In the second sentence, *by* is used to explain how they escaped (the means).

In formal English, *whom* is used after prepositions in the same way when referring to a person or another animate entity. However, in conversational English it is seldom used.

> The person *to whom* I spoke was the reference librarian. (formal)
> The person (*who*) *I talked to* was the reference librarian. (conversational)

In the second sentence, *who* is optional because it serves as the object of the preposition in the adjective clause.

*See unit 11 for additional information on prepositions.

---

1. *Whose* can also be preceded by a preposition, as in *Mr. Wilson, in whose name I am writing, requests that you contact him.*
2. In spoken English it is common to substitute *where* for *in* (*at, on,* etc.) *which* (place) and *when* for *on* (*in, at,* etc.) *which* (time). *This is the house where I was born. This is the date when the medicine expires.*

Reducing Relative Clauses

It is sometimes possible to shorten relative clauses by removing less essential information. Two examples of ways to reduce adjective clauses are discussed here.

One way is to eliminate *who, that, which + be,* unless *be* is followed by an adjective.

> Skydiving, (which is) a difficult and dangerous sport, is very popular with both men and women in the United States.
> The cloth is made from cotton (that is) imported from Central America.
> Bill, who is extremely tall, had to buy a special desk chair. (usually no reduction)

It is also possible to reduce adjective clauses containing verbs such as *want, wish, consist, state, know, hope.* This is done by removing the pronoun and changing the verb to V + *-ing.*

> The family, (which consisted) *consisting* of 10 members, had its own volleyball team.
> Lydia, (who wanted) *wanting* to be polite, let the others in line ahead of her.

Practice

Exercise

Circle the letter of the best answer.

1. Steel is combined with chromium to produce a noncorrosive substance _____ as stainless steel.

   a. it is known
   b. that is known
   c. who is known
   d. we know it

2. Harvard, _____ in 1636, is one of the most prestigious universities in the United States.

   a. founding
   b. founded
   c. it was founded
   d. that was founded

3. Gabriel García Márquez, a Colombian writer _____ book *One Hundred Years of Solitude* is among his most famous, won the Nobel Prize for literature in 1982.

   a. whose
   b. who's
   c. which wrote a book
   d. his

4. Jenny Churchill, _____, was born in the United States and married an Englishman.

   a. she was the mother of Winston Churchill
   b. the mother of Winston Churchill
   c. her son was Winston Churchill
   d. Winston Churchill was her son

5. The applause, _____ to build, brought the musician back on stage.

   a. started
   b. starting
   c. that starting
   d. which starting

6. We are investigating several species of plants in North America _____ can cause an allergic skin reaction in humans.

   a. they
   b. that they

   c. that
   d. who

7. A silo is a large cylindrical structure _____.

   a. by which crops are stored
   b. in which crops are stored

   c. where crops are stored there
   d. they store crops there

8. Barns _____ to store crops and house animals.

   a. built
   b. that are built

   c. being built
   d. are built

9. Garlic, _____ for its medicinal properties, is a bulbous plant related to the onion.

   a. it is often eaten
   b. which is often eaten

   c. that is often eaten
   d. we often eat it

10. Nathaniel Hawthorne, _____ for his novel *The Scarlet Letter,* did not begin to write seriously until he was in his forties.

    a. whose best known
    b. is best known

    c. best known
    d. which is best known

Final Test

Circle the letter of the best answer.

1. A tool _____ to a wall or another surface is called a trowel.

   a. that we apply plaster
   b. that plaster is applied

   c. whose plaster is applied
   d. with which plaster is applied

2. One of the fastest runners of all times is Jesse Owens, _____ three world records in one day.

   a. which broke
   b. who broke

   c. whose
   d. that broke

3. Horse saddles, _____ of leather, are sometimes elaborately tooled.

   a. are made
   b. that are made

   c. they make them
   d. made

4. Mount Vernon, _____, has been restored to its original colors.

   a. George Washington lived there
   b. whose former owner was George Washington

   c. the house where did live George Washington
   d. in which lived George Washington there

5. Writers can accurately describe objects _____ have never seen.
   - a. that
   - b. they
   - c. whose shapes
   - d. which

6. Animal lovers take care of stray dogs and cats _____ they feel responsible.
   - a. for which
   - b. which
   - c. that
   - d. who

7. Custard is an egg dessert _____ primarily of eggs, sugar, and milk.
   - a. consisting
   - b. consists
   - c. which consisting
   - d. that is consisted

8. The banjo is a stringed musical instrument _____ to Africa.
   - a. native
   - b. who is native
   - c. is native
   - d. it is native

Review Test

Circle the letter of the best answer.

1. A higher crime rate exists in cities _____ a large percentage of unemployed people.
   - a. having
   - b. in which have
   - c. which they have
   - d. where have

2. Actors, musicians, and athletes _____ have reached a certain level of success are among the highest paid professionals in the world.
   - a. whom
   - b. which
   - c. they
   - d. that

3. _____ recommend coffee for hyperactive children is interesting.
   - a. People
   - b. That people
   - c. Do people
   - d. If or not people

4. The cost of shipping a car is related to _____ .
   - a. how much does it weigh
   - b. how much weighs it
   - c. how much it is weighed
   - d. how much it weighs

5. A softbound book is a book _____ a light, flexible cardboard.
   - a. that cover is made of
   - b. whose cover is made of
   - c. which cover is made of
   - d. its cover is made of

6. Because no records were kept in certain rural areas, some elderly people do not know _____ born with certain birth defects.
   - a. whether or not they were
   - b. were they
   - c. if or not they were
   - d. if they

7. _____ is made from cellulose is a little-known fact.
   - a. Rayon
   - b. That rayon
   - c. Being rayon
   - d. Rayon it

8. Maryanne, _____ house we were staying, gave us a delicious lunch.

    a. at whose

    b. whose

    c. in which

    d. who

9. Rosemary, _____ she was late, took a shortcut to the dentist's office.

    a. knowing

    b. who knowing

    c. that knew

    d. knew

10. A sewing machine is a device _____ clothes are made.

    a. with which

    b. by which

    c. in which

    d. for which

Unit 15

If (Conditional) Clauses

Circle the best answer.

1. If you (go) (will go) to the kitchen, get me a glass of water.
2. If the train arrives on time, (I'll be) (I would be) home by noon.
3. If I (was) (were) you, I'd tell the truth.
4. This sailboat (will) (would) go faster if there were more wind.
5. If you had come sooner, you could (has) (have) eaten dinner with us.
6. If the video game (had) (has) been more challenging, we would have bought it.
7. If your fever (might) (should) get worse, call the doctor.
8. (If) (Should) a tornado come, go to the basement immediately.
9. (Were) (If) this well-known painting for sale, it would be worth close to a million dollars.
10. (Had the committee members) (The committee members had) all agreed, Sara would have been given the scholarship.
11. I won't lend you this money (if) (unless) you promise to pay it back.
12. (If you call) (Call) me and I'll give you directions to my house.

Explanation

If clauses are used in English to state a condition for the occurrence or existence of something. The condition is stated in the *if* clause. For example,

> If you mix sugar with water, the sugar will dissolve.
> If they don't get sun and water, plants will die.

In the first example, the sugar will dissolve but on the condition that you mix it with water. In the second example, it is a fact that plants will die without sun and water. In other words, in order to survive, they need sun and water.

Notice that the *if* clause does not need to come at the beginning of the sentence.

> Sugar will dissolve if you mix it with water.
> Plants will die if they don't get sun and water.

Types of *if* (Conditional) Clauses

Three common types of *if* (conditional) clauses are discussed in this unit.

Type 1

The first type of *if* clause concerns real events or situations. In the following examples, notice the tenses in both the *if* clause and the main clause.

> If you *go* to the store, *buy* me a soft drink. (present; imperative)
> If Paul *stops* by, he usually *gives* us the weather report. (present; present)
> If Michelle *calls,* I'*ll invite* her to the concert. (present; future)
> If Michelle *should call,* I'*ll invite* her to the concert. (modal; future)

In type 1, the *if* clause is often in the present tense and the main clause in the present, future, or imperative. In the second example, both clauses are in the present tense and have to do with a habitual activity. In the third example, it appears that the speaker is going to a concert and will invite Michelle under the condition that she calls. *Will* is used in the main clause. The modal *should* can be used in the *if* clause, as in the fourth example.

There is little difference in meaning between the third and fourth examples except that the use of *should* is considered more formal and may express more doubt about the possibility of Michelle's calling. It is incorrect to use the modal *might* instead of *should.*

>   **should**
> If Michelle ~~might~~ call, I'll invite her to the concert.

Past tense may also be used in type 1 *if* clauses.

> If Jeffrey left the house, his dog would follow/followed him.

Notice that *would* is used to indicate a habitual action in the past. (See unit 5.) The alternative, *followed,* also expresses a habitual action.

Type 2

The second type of *if* clause is concerned with hypothetical or unreal situations in the present. The *if* clause introduces the hypothetical condition. Notice the choice of tense.

> If I *had* the money, I *would* buy a motorcycle. (past tense; modal)
> If Eric *were* here, he *could* fix the plumbing. (past tense; modal)

In the first example, the hypothetical *if* clause is used because the speaker doesn't have the money but is imagining what he would do if he did. In the second example, Eric isn't present, but the speaker is hypothesizing what could occur if he were present.

Notice that in type 2, the *if* clause is in the past. Also, *were* is used in place of *was,* especially in formal situations. In the main clause the modals *would* or *could* are used.

In type 1 *if* clauses, *will* is not commonly used in the *if* clause.

>   **rains**
> If it ~~will rain~~ tomorrow, we can't play baseball.

Likewise, in type 2 *if* clauses, *would* is not used in the *if* clause.

>   **had**
> If I ~~would have~~ money, I'd invite you to dinner.

When *will* and *would* are used in the *if* clause, they have the meaning "be willing to," as in *If you will wash the dishes, I'll cook dinner.*

Type 3

The third type of *if* clause is concerned with hypothetical discussions about the past. Again notice the tenses in both clauses.

> If I *had known* you were sick, I *would have made* you some soup. (past perfect; modal-past)
> If you *had been* here yesterday, you *could have seen* Pam. (past perfect; modal-past)

Both examples refer to situations in the past, not the present. In the first example, the implication is that the speaker didn't know you were sick. Otherwise, the speaker would have made soup. In the second example, you were not here yesterday and thus didn't have the opportunity to see Pam.

In type 3, the *if* clause is in the past perfect, and the past forms of *would* and *could* (*would have seen, could have made*) are used in the main clause.

If Clauses and Inversion

The word *if* is helpful in recognizing the *if* clause. Unfortunately, it is not always present. Notice what happens in the following special cases.

Type 1: **should**

> If you should get a letter from Greece, give me a call.
> *Should* you get a letter from Greece, give me a call.

In the second example, *if* is eliminated, and the modal *should* and the subject *you* invert.

Type 2: **were**

> If you were taller, you could reach the light.
> *Were* you taller, you could reach the light.

Again, *if* is eliminated. This time, *were* inverts with the subject *you.*

> Note   In *if* clauses containing the modal *were to,* inversion can also occur. (Examples: *If you were to take the job, where would you live?* and *Were you to take the job, where would you live?*)

Type 3

> If I had agreed, Jim would have married me.
> *Had* I agreed, Jim would have married me.

In the second example *if* is eliminated, and *had* inverts with the subject *I.*

When inversion occurs, the meaning of the sentence does not change significantly. However, inversion is generally considered somewhat more formal.

Unless

Unless, which has a meaning similar to *if not,* can also be used in conditional clauses. The following two sentences have similar meanings.

> *If* it doesn*'t* rain, we'll go to the lake.
> *Unless* it rains, we'll go to the lake.

If so, if not, **and** *otherwise*

If so and *if not* are used to state a condition that is already known.

> "Jenny wants one of us to pick her up from basketball practice. I'm tired, but I'll go."
> "If so, I'll start dinner. If not, I can go and you can rest."

If so is short for *If you go,* and *If not* is short for *If you don't go. Otherwise* can be used instead of *If not.*

> "If so, I'll start dinner. *Otherwise,* I can go and you can rest."

If a condition doesn't exist or occur, *otherwise* is used to state the possible alternative or result.

> *If I fix the car,* we'll go on a picnic. *Otherwise,* we can go to the skating rink.
> *If there's tea,* I can have tea. *Otherwise,* I'll take water.

Practice

Exercise

Circle the letter of the best answer.

1. "Are you thinking about starting a vegetable garden?"

   "No, but if I _____ so many other obligations, I would definitely do it."

   a. didn't have   c. shouldn't have
   b. hadn't have   d. don't have

2. "Look at this rain!"

   "I hope it stops. _____, we'll have to camp somewhere else."

   a. If so   c. Unless
   b. If it didn't   d. Otherwise

3. "That's a nice computer."

   "If I had had more money, I _____ bought a faster one."

   a. will have   c. would
   b. would have   d. have

4. "My supervisor made me work overtime again."

   "If I were you, I _____ that job."

   a. would quit   c. must quit
   b. will quit   d. quit

5. "Thanks for your help."

   "_____ want more information, call again tomorrow."

   a. Were you   c. Might you
   b. Should you to   d. If you

6. "Remember the day I drove you to the airport?"

   "If you hadn't _____ me, I would have missed my plane."

   a. take   c. took
   b. taking   d. taken

7. "Sally finally got here from Chicago."

   "If she had come earlier, we _____ taken her to the historical district."

   a. would be   c. had have
   b. would have   d. would had

8. "I don't know whether to take that Spanish course or not."

   "If _____ you, I'd take it."

   a. I am   c. I had been you
   b. I will be   d. I were

9. "My car broke down when I was leaving for work, and I had to take the bus."

   "_____, we would have picked you up."

   a. Had we known   c. We had known
   b. If we have known   d. If we knew

10. "It's beginning to rain."

    "That's too bad. _____, we won't be able to go to the botanical gardens."

    a. If it stops   c. Unless it stops
    b. Should it stop   d. If it didn't stop

11. "Did you need help with your math last night?"

    "No. If I had, I _____ you."

    a. would call   c. would have called
    b. called   d. will call

12. "I'd really like some lunch, but I have so much work to do."

    "_____ what you want, and I can get it for you."

    a. Tell me   c. You will tell to me
    b. If you would say me   d. If you tell me

13. "I might need help changing a flat tire."

    "_____, I'd be glad to help."

    a. If you did   c. If so
    b. Unless you do   d. If not

14. "Moon is moving to his new apartment next Saturday."

    "_____ better, I won't be able to lift anything."

    a. Unless my back is   c. Should my back be
    b. If my back is   d. Shouldn't my back be

15. "Did you go to the art fair?"

"No. We would have, _____ nicer."

   a. had the weather been
   b. if the weather has been
   c. would the weather have been
   d. if the weather might be

Final Test

Study the following sentences. Decide if the italicized portion of the sentence is *correct* (C) or *incorrect* (I). Circle your answer.

1. If a drop of oil is placed in a glass of water, it *would* float to the top.   **C I**

2. The car would have survived the tornado, *had it been parked* on the other side of the road.   **C I**

3. Should there be a tie for first place in the competition, a runoff will be held. *Otherwise,* the winner will be announced tomorrow.   **C I**

4. If interest rates *hadn't been lowered,* many couples wouldn't have been able to purchase a new home.   **C I**

5. Hypothetically, *were these documents falsified,* serious legal consequences could occur.   **C I**

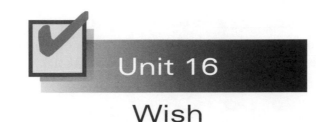

Unit 16

Wish

Circle the letter of the best answer.

1. "I think Kevin is sometimes very shy."

   "Me, too. I wish he _____ a little more outgoing."

   a. has been   c. will be

   b. were   d. is

2. "I need to pick up a pack of cigarettes from the store."

   "I wish you _____ smoking."

   a. would stop   c. have stopped

   b. stop   d. will stop

3. "Did you see Monica before she left for Brazil?"

   "No. I wish I _____ her."

   a. saw   c. have seen

   b. would see   d. had seen

4. "Would you like to go to the movies tonight?"

   "I wish I _____ , but I have to study for a test."

   a. had   c. would

   b. could   d. did

5. "Did you go to Sweden last January?"

   "Yes, but I wish I _____ in May when it was hotter."

   a. have gone   c. had gone

   b. went   d. go

Explanation

In English, the verb *wish* is used to express desire. *Wish* is commonly followed by a *that* clause; however, the word *that* is optional and is generally omitted. Like certain types of *if* clauses, wishes are considered to be hypothetical or unreal by English speakers. Thus, *wish* is often accompanied by past tense, past perfect tense, *would,* and *could.*

Three types of desire can be expressed by the verb *wish.*

Type 1

The first type is a desire for something to happen, a desire for an event or a change to occur in the future, or a desire to be able to do something.[1]

> Jack is lonely and wishes (that) his parents *would* visit.
> We wish (that) we *would/could* see you more in the future.
> I wish I *could* play the piano.

Notice that *would* and *could* are always used rather than present tense, *will* or *can,* which would be incorrect.

> would
> I wish someone ~~will~~ give me a million dollars.

> could
> We wish we ~~can~~ speak English better.

This type of wish is also used to make a request.

> I wish (that) you *would* play the piano for us.
> I wish you *would* stop complaining.

Type 2

The second type of desire expressed by *wish* is a desire for the existence of something—a changed state, a characteristic, a habitual occurrence, etc.—or a desire for something to be happening at the present time.

> Noah wishes he *knew* you.
> I wish I *had* green eyes.
> I wish it *were* Friday. (informal: I *wish* it was Friday.)
> We wish you *visited* more often.
> Everybody wishes the sun *were shining.* (now)

Notice that *wish* is followed by the past tense and that in formal English *were* instead of *was* is used.

It is not correct to use present tense in this second type.

> had
> I wish I ~~have~~ a car of my own.

---

1. The verb *hope* is used with *will* to express a desire or an expectation for the future, as in *I hope (that) the train will be on time; I hope you win.*

Type 3

The third type of *wish* expresses regret about the *past.*

> I wish I *had graduated* from high school.[2]
> Kathy will wish she *hadn't married* so young.
> We wished we *hadn't been convinced* to buy that painting. (passive)
> I wish you *could have come* with us.

In this type, *wish* is followed by the past perfect tense rather than the past tense. Notice that the verb *wish* need not occur in past tense but the situation must always refer to the past.

Practice

Exercise

Circle the letter of the best answer.

1. "Scott has three sisters, doesn't he?"

   "No wonder he wishes he _____ a brother."

   a. had   c. will have
   b. have   d. can have

2. "I hear that the Jenkinses lost their suitcases on vacation."

   "I bet now they wish they _____."

   a. have never gone   c. never went
   b. never go   d. had never gone

3. "My daughter wants to take horseback riding lessons."

   "Many children wish they _____ that."

   a. can do   c. could do
   b. will do   d. do

4. "So, the driver was telling the truth about the accident."

   "I wish I _____ her."

   a. believe   c. have believed
   b. would believe   d. had believed

5. "I've got to finish writing this report."

   "I wish you _____ so busy."

   a. weren't   c. haven't been
   b. aren't   d. won't be

---

2. In informal English, it is also possible to say, "*I wish I would have graduated* from high school" or "*Kathy will wish she wouldn't have married* so young."

6. "What do you want, Mom?"

"Billy, I wish you _____ that music."

a. turn down
b. have turned down
c. would turn down
d. having turned down

7. "Did you order copies of your wedding pictures?"

"I only ordered one copy, but now I wish I _____ two."

a. had ordered
b. order
c. have ordered
d. would ordered

8. "Did you ever finish high school?"

"No, I didn't. But I wish I _____."

a. have
b. had
c. will
d. were

9. "Maybe Paula will bring us good news about the test results."

"I wish she _____."

a. does
b. will
c. brings it
d. would

10. "It's too bad Andy is moving to Arizona."

"I wish it _____ so far away."

a. weren't
b. won't be
c. couldn't be
d. isn't

Final Test

Study the following sentences. Decide if the italicized portion of the sentence is *correct* (C) or *incorrect* (I). Circle your answer.

1. Children sometimes wish they *can do* things their older brothers and sisters do.   C   I

2. Living near the ocean is nice, but we wish the weather *weren't* so humid.   C   I

3. I wish the neighbors *cut down* that dead tree.   C   I

4. During the test tomorrow we will wish we *had studied* harder.   C   I

5. Joel now wishes he *hasn't broken* his engagement with Liza.   C   I

Review Test

Circle the letter of the best answer.

1. "Why did you only stay a week in San Francisco?"

   "If I _____ more time, I would have stayed longer."

   a. had had
   b. would have
   c. had
   d. have

2. "I can't go biking this afternoon because I have a test."

   "_____ change your mind, give me a call."

   a. Might you
   b. Were you
   c. Should you
   d. Would you

3. "Do you want anything from the store?"

   "If they sell candied popcorn, get me a bag. _____, get me some potato chips."

   a. Otherwise
   b. If so
   c. If no
   d. If don't

4. "Did you see Florence before you left Italy?"

   "No, but I wish we _____."

   a. saw it
   b. will
   c. would
   d. had

5. "Gary asked me to marry him."

   "If I were you, I _____ about it seriously."

   a. think
   b. would thought
   c. would think
   d. will think

6. "Did you call the dentist for an appointment yet?"

   "_____ me the telephone number and I'll call him now."

   a. If you give
   b. Give
   c. If you gave
   d. Unless you give

7. "Phoebe is such a friendly person."

   "Yes. I wish she _____ more often."

   a. would drop by   c. will drop
   b. would dropped by   d. drops

8. "Did you go hiking in the mountains last week?"

   "No. _____ warmer, we would have gone."

   a. Had the weather been   c. If the weather is
   b. If the weather has been d. Would the weather be

9. "Are you coming to the gym?"

   "I wish I _____, but I have to work."

   a. had   c. will
   b. could   d. could have

10. "The weather is terrible."

    "It is so hot that I wish I _____ at the beach right now."

    a. would be   c. were
    b. would have been   d. had been

Unit 17

Negative Adverbs

Circle the letter of the best answer.

1. "This store has such high prices."

   "I agree. Never again _____ here."
   - a. I will shop
   - b. will I shop
   - c. I do shop
   - d. shop I

2. "Is this copy machine often in need of repair?"

   "No. _____ serious repair problems."
   - a. Hardly ever don't we expect
   - b. We expect hardly ever
   - c. Hardly ever we expect
   - d. Hardly ever do we expect

3. "I can't see the band very well from here."

   "_____."
   - a. Neither can't I
   - b. Neither I can
   - c. I can't neither
   - d. Neither can I

4. Not until the early 1900s _____ to vote in the United States.
   - a. women were allowed
   - b. were women allowed
   - c. they allowed women
   - d. when women were allowed

5. Only recently _____ a favorite sport in the United States.
   - a. has snowboarding become
   - b. has become snowboarding
   - c. snowboarding becomes
   - d. snowboarding has become

Explanation

Negative Adverbs and Inversion

In English there is a group of negative adverbs that generally refer to time or place, such as *never, no longer,* or *nowhere.* When these adverbs occur before the subject of a sentence, they require subject-auxiliary or *be* inversion.

Never *has there* been such controversy over road construction.

   compared to

There has never been such controversy over road construction.
(Notice that *there* functions as the subject for purposes of inversion.)

No longer *will the city tolerate graffiti.*

   compared to

The city will no longer tolerate graffiti.

Nowhere in city hall *is a person* so highly regarded as the mayor's secretary.

   compared to

No person in city hall is so highly regarded as the mayor's secretary.
(Notice that the original sentence had to be altered.)

Almost never do you see dial phones anymore.

   compared to

You almost never see dial phones anymore.

In the last example, it is necessary to add the auxiliary *do*. It would be incorrect in English to invert the subject with the verb *see*.

$$\overset{do\ you\ see}{\text{Almost never \sout{see you} dial phones anymore.}}$$

The following is a list of negative adverbs of time and place that, when they occur at the beginning of a sentence, require subject-auxiliary inversion.

Never	Almost never	Hardly ever
Never again	Seldom	Only then
No longer	Rarely (ever)	Not until
At no time	Rarely if ever	No sooner
No way[1]	Scarcely ever	
Nowhere	Barely ever	

1. *No way* is used in conversational English but generally not in formal English, e.g., *No way are we gonna finish this homework by tomorrow. No way am I taking a physics class.*

Since these adverbs are already considered negative, it is incorrect to use them with a negative auxiliary or verb.

$$\overset{does}{\text{At no time \sout{doesn't} the park allow campers to feed the bears.}}$$

So, neither, nor, as

In conversation, subject-auxiliary or *be* inversion occurs commonly in short answers with *neither (nor)* and *so*. It also occurs in more formal English with *as,* which has the same meaning as *so.* (See the last set of examples.) Notice here, however, that *so* is preceded by *and.*

> "I don't have any money."
> "Neither *do I.*" or "Nor *do I.*"

> "I've got some money."
> "So *do I.*"

> Jonathan reads frequently, and *so do his friends.*
> Jonathan reads frequently, *as do his friends.* (formal)

Only, not only . . . (but also)

Only . . . and *Not only . . . (but also)* are also followed by subject-auxiliary or *be* inversion.

> *Only* under certain atmospheric conditions *is there* a chance of a tornado.
> *Not only does the university offer* health benefits to employees, but it also offers free life insurance.

Practice

Exercise

Circle the letter of the best answer.

1. "This is one of the oldest trees in the world."

   "_____ such a big tree."
   - a. Never I have seen
   - b. I haven't never seen
   - c. Never have I seen
   - d. I have seen never

2. "What happened to Judy's new truck?"

   "No sooner _____ it than someone ran into her."
   - a. had she bought
   - b. she bought
   - c. did she bought
   - d. she had bought

3. "I would like to apply for the sales position you advertised."

   "I'm sorry. No longer _____ applications for that position."
   - a. are taking we
   - b. we are taking
   - c. are we taking
   - d. we taking

4. Amoebas reproduce by dividing _____.
   - a. and other protozoans
   - b. as do other protozoans
   - c. other protozoans do too
   - d. and so other protozoans

5. _____ a higher concentration of people than in Tokyo and Mexico City.

    a. Nowhere there is   c. Nowhere is there

    b. Nowhere is   d. Nowhere there isn't

6. "Did you like your trip to Niagara Falls?"

    "It was beautiful. _____ such a spectacular sight."

    a. You hardly ever see   c. Hardly ever you do see

    b. Hardly ever you see   d. You see hardly ever

7. "Can children swim in this pool?"

    "Yes. However, at no time _____ alone."

    a. shouldn't they swim   c. should swim they

    b. they should swim   d. should they swim

8. Only during the early twentieth century _____ in the United States.

    a. liquor was prohibited   c. when liquor was prohibited

    b. that liquor was prohibited   d. was liquor prohibited

9. "I don't like this tossed salad very well."

    "Nor _____."

    a. I do   c. do I

    b. I do either   d. I like it either

10. Not only _____, but he also plays the piano and writes his own songs.

    a. does Jeremy sing   c. if Jeremy sings

    b. Jeremy sings   d. sings Jeremy

Final Test

Study the following sentences. Decide if the italicized portion of the sentence is *correct* (C) or *incorrect* (I). Circle your answer.

1. Nowhere *mosquitoes are* more prevalent than in warm, swampy places.   **C** **I**

2. Only when the ground is kept moist *will these grass seeds* germinate.   **C** **I**

3. Not until the 1960s *women in the United States were* given equal employment rights as men.   **C** **I**

4. The bank *will no longer offer* a free checking service.   **C** **I**

5. Rarely *do professional boxers remain* active beyond the age of thirty-five.   **C** **I**

Unit 18

That Clauses in the Subjunctive (Bare Infinitive)

Pretest

Circle the letter of the best answer.

1. "Doctor, what is your opinion about Bob's condition?"

    "I recommend _____ as much as possible."

    a. him to rest
    b. him rest
    c. that he rests
    d. that he rest

2. "Why does Ted need a tutor?"

    "Because it's important _____ on his entrance exam next month."

    a. that he do well
    b. he well does
    c. for him do well
    d. that he will do well

3. "Where's Luke?"

    "He's so good with computers that his supervisor requested _____ to Kansas City for more training."

    a. that he went
    b. that he goes
    c. that he will go
    d. that he go

4. "Did you hear that Nicole's plane is canceled in Chicago?"

    "Yes. We suggested that she _____ a train."

    a. her to take
    b. take
    c. took
    d. would take

5. "Please take this seat."

    "No, I insist on _____."

    a. you take it
    b. your taking it
    c. you will take it
    d. you to take it

Explanation

In English a group of verbs and adjectives that are used to recommend, suggest, request, demand, express urgency or necessity, etc., are commonly followed by a *that* clause containing the subjunctive (bare infinitive (V)). These are not very common in casual speech but may be used by persons in authority.

> I recommend that your daughter *stop* drinking. (bare infinitive (V))
> It is necessary that you *be* here on time. (bare infinitive (V))
> The Smiths insisted that we *stay* for dinner. (bare infinitive (V))

Notice that in the first example, the verb *stop* does not contain the third person singular (*stops*) but instead occurs in the subjunctive or bare infinitive form (*stop*). Likewise, in the second example, the subjunctive *be* is used, rather than the second person *are*.

In the third example, even though the main verb (*insisted*) is in the past, the *that* clause that follows still contains the bare infinitive rather than the past tense form of the verb (*stayed*).

The following two sentences are, therefore, incorrect in formal English.

> **have**
> It is important that Pat ~~has~~ a business degree for her job.

> **be**
> The doctor recommended that the pregnant woman ~~was~~ taken to the hospital immediately.

The Subjunctive, Gerunds, and Infinitives

Some verbs and adjectives that are followed by a *that* clause can also be followed by a gerund or an infinitive. (See the list below.) For example, it is correct to say:

> We insisted that he take his time.
> We insisted on his taking his time.

> I asked that she not go.
> I asked her not to go.

> It's important that we be there.
> It's important for us to be there.

This is generally not true of other verbs such as *suggest* and *recommend*. In formal written English, it is correct to say:

> The editor *suggested* that the author *revise* portions of the manuscript.

But it is not usually considered correct to say:

> **that I revise**
> The editor suggested ~~for me to revise~~ portions of the manuscript.

To make the bare infinitive negative, *not* is used before the bare infinitive.

> The nurses requested that the patient *not* get out of bed by himself.

That *Clauses Containing the Bare Infinitive**	Infinitive Form	Gerund Form
I suggest that he go.		
recommend		
demand		
request		
insist		I insist on his going.
propose		
I urge that he go.*	I urge him to go.	
ask*	ask	
require	require	
prefer	prefer	
It is important that he go.	It is important for him to go.	
urgent	urgent	
necessary	necessary	
essential	essential	
imperative	imperative	

*These verbs are followed by an obligatory *that*. Otherwise, *that* is optional.

Practice

Exercise

Circle the letter of the best answer.

1. "The telephone company is threatening to cut off our service."

   "It's urgent _____ the bill immediately."

   a. that we pay   c. for us pay

   b. us to pay   d. that we have to pay

2. "What did the doctor tell Rachel about her health?"

   "He recommended _____ less."

   a. that she worked   c. her work

   b. that she work   d. that she working

3. "Should I tell Pierre about the broken window?"

   "Yes. It's necessary _____ it before it rains."

   a. that he fixes   c. his fixing

   b. that he fix   d. he fixes

4. "We just got a letter from Ron."

   "It's surprising _____ to you after all these years."

   a. that he still write   c. that still is writing

   b. that he still writes   d. that he still writing

5. "What did the school coaches tell Chuck?"

   "They insisted _____ a haircut."

   a. that he got   c. he get
   b. that he gets   d. him to get

6. "Who do you think should work on the construction project?"

   "I recommend _____ the head engineer."

   a. for Victoria be   c. that Victoria is
   b. that Victoria be   d. Victoria being

7. "Should I begin typing these letters?"

   "I suggest _____ the bookkeeping first."

   a. you finished   c. you finish
   b. you to finish   d. you will finish

8. "Did you father give you that watch?"

   "Yes. He insisted _____ it."

   a. that I took   c. on my taking
   b. I will take   d. for me to take

9. "Have you received the shipment of bicycles yet?"

   "No, but it's possible that it _____ in a few days."

   a. will come   c. come
   b. comes   d. has come

10. "Kristin practices the piano at six in the morning."

    "We asked _____, but she won't."

    a. that she stops   c. her to stop
    b. her stopping   d. for her stop

Final Test

Study the following sentences. Decide if the italicized portion of the sentence is *correct* (C) or *incorrect* (I). Circle your answer.

1. Doctors recommend that, if possible, a pregnant mother *not take* medicine.   **C   I**

2. Many older citizens have requested that social security *be made* a national priority.   **C   I**

3. The mayor thinks it is imperative that the city *will repair* the city streets soon.   **C   I**

4. Laws now insist *on that* drunk drivers pay stiff fines and go to jail.   **C   I**

5. City residents prefer that bus stops be close to their home.   **C   I**

Review Test

Circle the letter of the best answer.

1. "The weather seems very dry here."

   "Seldom _____ in this area."

   a. it rains

   b. does it rain

   c. rains it

   d. it does rain

2. "They suggested that we _____ handicrafts on our vacation in New Mexico."

   a. buy

   b. bought

   c. to buy

   d. will buy

3. Only in the last few years _____ to use cell phones exclusively.

   a. have begun people

   b. when people began

   c. have people begun

   d. people have begun

4. "What did the teacher tell you?"

   "She recommended _____ with an American family to improve my English."

   a. that I live

   b. me living

   c. me to live

   d. living for me

5. "When should we ask Eric to come to work?"

   "Why don't we propose _____ here about 7:30?"

   a. that he be

   b. that he will be

   c. him to be

   d. him being

6. "I don't like tofu very much."

   "That's not surprising. _____."

   a. Neither I do

   b. Neither do I

   c. I don't neither

   d. Neither don't I

7. What a beautiful ring! Never _____ such an intricate design.

    a. have seen I
            c. I have seen

    b. have I seen
            d. I haven't seen

8. "You got home late last night."

   "The Morgans insisted _____ for dinner."

    a. on our staying
            c. that we were staying

    b. for us to stay
            d. about us staying

9. "Did your wife agree to throw out that horrible chair?"

   "I asked _____, but she wouldn't."

    a. that she throws it out
            c. that she threw it out

    b. her throw it out
            d. her to do it

10. Hurricanes have a center of low pressure _____.

    a. as do tornadoes
            c. so tornadoes do

    b. and tornadoes
            d. so tornadoes do too

Examinations

The following four examinations test the major grammar points in units 1–18. After taking one test, review the grammar points you haven't thoroughly mastered before going on to the next test.

— Exam 1 —

Part 1

Circle the letter of the best answer.

1. Orlando, a city in Florida, _____ for its main attraction—Disney World.
   - a. which is well known
   - b. well known
   - c. and well known
   - d. is well known

2. _____ evening soap operas such as *Dallas* began to grow popular among TV viewers.
   - a. In the 1970s
   - b. At the 1970s
   - c. In 1970s
   - d. On the 1970s

3. The California condor, which is among _____, has a wingspan of nearly ten feet.
   - a. the largest birds of the world
   - b. the largest birds in the world
   - c. the most large birds of the world
   - d. the most large birds in the world

4. Invasive plants _____ so that native plants can take their place.
   - a. destroyed
   - b. being destroyed
   - c. are destroying
   - d. are being destroyed

5. Owls have a strong beak and sharp talons _____ mice and other small prey.
   - a. used for catching
   - b. which used to catch
   - c. their use is to catch
   - d. that they are used for catching

6. The lower interest rates fall, _____ for larger items such as cars and homes.
   - a. more consumers shop
   - b. the more consumers shop
   - c. there are more consumer shopping
   - d. consumers shop more

7. If home insulation _____ to prevent the passage of air, it will also prevent the passage of sound.

   a. used   c. is used

   b. be used   d. were used

8. _____ turn color and fall to the ground is a sign of autumn.

   a. That leaves   c. When leaves

   b. Leaves   d. If leaves

9. Experiments on mental patients took place in the 1950s but _____ by the U.S. Supreme Court.

   a. have since been banned   c. have since banned

   b. are since banned   d. had since been banned

10. Invertebrates _____ a backbone.

   a. which don't have   c. no have

   b. not have   d. don't have

11. In the southwestern part of the United States, there are many abandoned mining towns built _____ the nineteenth century.

   a. at   c. on

   b. in   d. by

12. Only when they are injured _____.

   a. will some animals attack a human being   c. some animals will attack a human being

   b. a human being will be attacked by some animals   d. that some animals attack a human being

13. The Amish, who settled largely in Pennsylvania, speak a dialect of Swiss German, _____.

   a. their ancestors too   c. so did their ancestors

   b. as did their ancestors   d. and their ancestors

14. _____ in office, he possibly would have run for the presidency for a fifth time.

   a. Franklin D. Roosevelt died   c. Had Franklin D. Roosevelt not died

   b. If Franklin D. Roosevelt had died   d. Franklin D. Roosevelt died

15. Those _____ the Nobel Prize are invited by the Swedish government to attend a ceremony in Stockholm.

   a. who win   c. which win

   b. won   d. have won

Part 2

Circle the italicized portion of the sentence that is *incorrect*.

1. Clay *that* *has been* heated or fired in a kiln cannot *to be softened* again.

2. *Improperly* made clothing *are* usually not *discarded* but instead *given away*.

3. *The* percentage of *tax* levied on *imported* goods may be related to the *availableness* of those goods nationally.

4. Georgia O'Keeffe was *not only* a model for her photographer husband Alfred Stieglitz *but also* an *extremely* gifted *painting*.

5. *A* large *amount* of the nation's waterways *have been polluted by* factory waste, ships, and oil spills.

6. *The* staghorn fern belongs to a class of *plant that* do not *reproduce* by seeds but by spores.

7. *In* the mid-1800s, gold was *discover* in California, and a steady migration of people quickly *populated the* region.

8. An Olympic gold medal was *won* by *the* U.S. women's soccer team, *a* accomplishment *that surprised* many.

9. In response *to energy crisis*, Japanese *automobile* companies began making *smaller,* more fuel-*efficient* cars.

10. It *is thought* that more *as* 450 million people *will speak* English *by* the end of this decade.

11. In order for a bike *to function well,* it must be *lubricated from time and time*.

12. Merchants use *cautious* in accusing someone of robbery since they may *be sued if the* person is innocent.

13. Silk, a *lightly* material made from the cocoon of silkworms, is difficult *to produce* and *more costly than* cotton or rayon.

14. Helen Keller, *who* was both blind and *deaf, overcome* her *limitations* with the help of her teacher, Anne Sullivan.

15. *An* employee who *wants* permission *for going* on vacation often *must make* a request in advance.

16. A *delay* in delivery *can* cause *milk spoil*.

17. *Fresh* lakes and *river provide* a source of income to *the* North American fisher.

18. *A* person's *height* is *measured* in *feets* rather than in yards.

19. A telephone poll is *an* interview *that* consists *on* a series of questions on a *timely* topic.

20. *Approximately* 30 percent of *a* worker's income *are paid* in taxes and social security to *the* federal government.

21. *If an* object *will move* away from a nearsighted person, *it* becomes blurry.

22. Mach 1 is a *measurement used* to indicate that an object can travel *so* fast as *the* speed of sound.

23. *From* childhood Picasso *showed* a strong interest *to paint* that *remained* with him throughout his life.

24. The novel *The Dollmaker* concerns *about* a woman *who makes* dolls from wood in order *to support* her family during World War II.

25. The *Titanic,* a large *passenger* ship, *it sank* en route *from Europe to* North America after it hit an iceberg.

— Exam 2 —

Circle the letter of the best answer.

1. "What do you think of the book?"

   "_____ the ones in the series, it was the most interesting."

   a. From all   c. All of

   b. All   d. Of all

2. "Are you a good dancer?"

   "I don't dance _____."

   a. exceptional good   c. exceptionally well

   b. exceptionally good   d. exceptional well

3. "What did the surgeon tell Elizabeth?"

   "He recommended _____ a knee operation."

   a. that she have   c. her have

   b. she has   d. that she will have

4. "Is Ashley still here?"

   "No. She was the first _____."

   a. leaving   c. to leave

   b. that she left   d. in leaving

5. "My car needs an oil change."

   "_____ the mechanic do it."

   a. Get   c. Ask

   b. Have   d. Tell

6. "Do you like the new miniseries on TV?"

   "My kids like it, but I find it a little _____."

   a. boring   c. boredom

   b. bored   d. bore

7. "What's wrong with your smoke alarm?"

   "The battery needs _____."

   a. to replace   c. to be replace

   b. replacing   d. replace

8. "When is George going into the army?"

   "He _____ to go tomorrow."

   a. should   c. have

   b. must   d. is

9. "How about going to a movie or the comedy club?"

"OK, but I'd rather _____ to the comedy club."

a. not go   c. not to go

b. to not go   d. don't go

10. "What is that magazine you're reading?"

"It concerns _____ your money."

a. investing   c. about investing

b. to invest   d. with investing

11. "Are you still employed at the post office?"

"Yes. I _____ there since 1982."

a. had been working   c. have working

b. worked   d. have been working

12. "Do you know the Miltons?"

"Yes. They're _____ nice people."

a. so   c. such

b. such a   d. so nice a

13. "When you were living out west, were there a lot of deer?"

"Yes, but _____ any."

a. hardly ever we saw   c. hardly ever did we saw

b. we saw hardly ever   d. we hardly ever saw

14. "Raul gets better grades than his sister."

"_____, his sister is more musical."

a. On contrast   c. In the other hand

b. On the contrary   d. In contrast

15. "Did you sell your car yet?"

"No, but there's a woman who is _____ in buying it."

a. definitely interested   c. definitely interesting

b. definite interested   d. interested definitely

16. "Is your dog afraid of me?"

"A little. It's not used to _____."

a. be petted   c. being petted

b. petting   d. pet

17. "How old are you?"

"I'm _____ you are."

a. the same old as   c. the same age as

b. as same age as   d. as same old as

18. "Did you order extra photographs?"

    "No, I didn't, but now I wish I _____."

    a. ordered them   c. had

    b. have ordered them   d. had ordered

19. "Did you see the meteor shower last night?"

    "I didn't even _____ about it."

    a. know   c. known

    b. knew   d. had known

20. "You look exhausted."

    "I'm _____ that I can't keep my eyes open."

    a. so tired   c. so much

    b. such a   d. very tired

21. "Are you going to quit your job?"

    "I don't know. I _____ to."

    a. might   c. could

    b. ought   d. may

22. "Your plane is eight hours late."

    "Never again _____ on a holiday weekend."

    a. will travel I   c. will I travel

    b. I will travel   d. I won't travel

23. "Jennifer's band was on TV last night."

    "_____, we would have watched her."

    a. Had we known   c. If we have known

    b. We had known   d. If we did know

24. "Christine is moving to Los Angeles."

    "_____ will make everyone sad."

    a. Her leaving   c. She leaving

    b. She leaves   d. For her leaving

25. "Some teenagers own cars when they're still in high school."

    "Our son's friend _____ one."

    a. is buying   c. is bought

    b. buys   d. have bought

26. "When are you leaving for South Carolina?"

    "I think I'll go _____ June 11."

    a. at   c. between

    b. in   d. on

27. "How is Holly's fever?"

    "_____ it get worse, we'll take her to the doctor."

    a. Should   c. Might
    b. If   d. Unless

28. "They say we might get a two-year contract."

    "I wish it _____ more certain."

    a. were   c. has been
    b. is   d. will be

29. "Did you take your car to the repair shop?"

    "Yes. It _____ right now."

    a. is being fixed   c. will fix
    b. is fixing   d. is to be fix

30. "Where did Julie get those old newspapers?"

    "I'm not sure. She _____ them in the basement."

    a. could have found   c. could have finded
    b. could have find   d. could find

31. "Is the old fence still standing?"

    "No. It _____ a year ago."

    a. has fallen down   c. fell down
    b. was fallen down   d. had fell down

32. "Do you want to go to the midnight movie?"

    "I'm so tired that I really _____ to go to bed."

    a. must   c. should
    b. have   d. will

33. "How did Jamie find out she was expecting twins?"

    "She _____ by her midwife."

    a. told   c. has told
    b. was told   d. was telling

34. "What a beautiful area!"

    "This is the park _____ the best."

    a. where I like   c. in which I like
    b. that I like   d. I like it

35. "My shirt is torn."

    "_____ me a needle and thread, and I'll fix it for you."

    a. If you bring   c. If you brought
    b. Bring   d. Should you bring

36. "I passed the calculus exam!"

    "Congratulations. _____ a lot before you took it?"

    a. Have you studied   c. Did you studied
    b. Had you studied   d. Do you study

37. "Did you find anything with your metal detector?"

    "_____ gold coins."

    a. A few   c. A few of
    b. A little   d. A few number of

38. "Are you and Toni friends?"

    "I've known her _____ I was in first grade."

    a. for   c. until
    b. since   d. during

39. "Food is getting so expensive."

    "Yes. You get _____ for your money now."

    a. so few   c. so less
    b. so little   d. so fewer

40. "Our baseball team won the state championship."

    "I heard. _____ the Panthers was a surprise."

    a. That they beat   c. They beat
    b. That they were beaten   d. They beating

— Exam 3 —

Part 1

Circle the letter of the best answer.

1. Coffee beans are picked by hand and then _____.

    a. are sorting   c. sorted
    b. we sorted them   d. are being sorted

2. _____ twenty-first century, immigrants to North America had entered from nearly every country.

    a. The   c. The beginning of the
    b. By the   d. At the

3. Now doctors frequently operate _____ patients on an outpatient basis.

    a. on   c. to
    b. in   d. at

4. The term *hybrid* commonly refers to a plant _____ from two different species of plants.

    a. creating   c. created
    b. that creates   d. was created

5. Only one species of snake in Michigan _____ poisonous—the massasauga rattler.

    a. it is   c. is
    b. that is   d. are

6. In the 1960s, some _____ moved to Canada to show their opposition to the Vietnam War.

    a. draft resisters   c. draft resisters who
    b. draft resisters which   d. draft resisters they

7. _____ manufacturing industry has been in decline.

    a. The steel   c. Steel
    b. A steel   d. That the steel

8. No human being _____ alone to the North Pole until 1984.

    a. has ever traveled   c. did ever travel
    b. had ever traveled   d. had ever travel

9. The higher the altitude, _____ .

    a. the thinner the air will become   c. thinner air will be there
    b. there will be thinner air   d. the air will become thinner

10. _____ earn money, they are subject to income tax under federal law.

    a. Children   c. Should children
    b. Children who   d. Were children to

11. Walt Disney, _____ cartoon characters are known throughout the world, is recognized as one of the greatest producers of animated films.

    a. whose   c. that
    b. his   d. which

12. Nowhere in the northern section of the United States _____ for growing citrus crops.

    a. the climate is suitable   c. is the climate suitably
    b. is the climate suitable   d. the climate isn't suitable

13. _____ , but he also took an interest in the flight of birds.

    a. Not only did Rembrandt paint   c. Rembrandt not only did paint
    b. Not only did Rembrandt painted   d. Not only Rembrandt painted

14. Polls predict in advance _____ .
   a. what the results of an election will be
   b. what will be the results of an election
   c. the results of an election will be
   d. that the results of an election will be

15. _____ erupt, they can change weather conditions.
   a. If volcanoes
   b. If volcanoes might
   c. If volcanoes will
   d. Might volcanoes

Part 2

Circle the italicized portion of the sentence that is *incorrect*.

1. Parents often *encourage* their children *attend* college, *especially if* they went to college *themselves*.

2. Some of the most *architecturally significance* private homes in the United States *were designed by* Frank Lloyd Wright.

3. *It estimated* that, because of *severe* weather, citrus fruit *will be more costly* for consumers this year.

4. *Not until* recently *have computers been* considered *as* a *necessity*.

5. In the Revolutionary War, *which* took place *from 1775 to 1783*, British soldiers used *conventionally* military tactics against their American *adversaries*.

6. Some city *ordinance* prevent drivers from *parking on* the streets after *a* specified hour.

7. The law states that *a* imported car *must be equipped* with specified *safety* features on *entering* the United States.

8. Diamonds, *the* most *expensive* of *all* precious stones, *are measure* in carats.

9. John Glenn, one of the first *astronauts to explore* outer space, later *become a* U.S. senator.

10. Hardwood furniture *built* by expert woodworkers can be *tasteful, elegance,* and *enduring*.

11. *Pass* a driver's test is a *necessary* requirement for those people *wanting to drive* a motor vehicle.

12. *Film* is *developed* in a room *that* is totally *darkness*.

13. *The* topic of violence in the movies *have* been *widely discussed* in this country.

14. *A* philanthropist is *a* person *who donates generously money* to individuals and institutions.

15. New *educated* materials in a variety of fields *are displayed yearly* at teachers' conventions.

16. Sometimes *a* young male bird, *alike its* mother, will have brown or gray feathers rather than *brightly colored* ones.

17. Banks *will* usually issue a four-*years* loan to *an* employed customer *wishing* to purchase a car.

18. Outside of class, professors read *extensively,* plan lectures, and *meet* with colleagues *to discuss* their *researches*.

19. *Unless* they are on a leash, some dogs *may unexpectedly* bite *the* strangers.

20. Some people *grow so tall that* their *healthy becomes* endangered.

21. Lack of *experience* causes drivers who are not used to *driving* on ice *lose* control of *their* vehicle.

22. Even though driving laws are *fairly* consistent *from state to state,* it is important for drivers *be aware* of any *discrepancy* when they enter a new state.

23. Water pipes *made of* plastic are *durable* and *relative* inexpensive *to produce.*

24. Many adults *who do not qualify* for occupations because they lack computer skills *had recently returned* to school for *additional* training.

25. Among *other* reasons, the Humane Society was established *to shelter* animals, educate animal owners, and *influenced* legislation regarding *the* protection of animals.

— Exam 4 —

Circle the letter of the best answer.

1. "Is the party almost over?"

    "I think so. A lot of people _____ to leave."

    a. is beginning
    b. are beginning
    c. begin
    d. have beginning

2. "When do you work now?"

    "Usually _____ the afternoon."

    a. at
    b. during
    c. to
    d. on

3. "You look tired."

    "I am. I have _____ to do."

    a. too many homeworks
    b. too much homeworks
    c. much too many homework
    d. too many homework assignments

4. "Which car is winning the race?"

    "They are moving so _____ I can hardly see them."

    a. fastly
    b. quickly
    c. rapid
    d. much quickly

5. "Did you have bad weather on the ship?"

    "Yes. We had _____ rain than the weather report had predicted."

    a. a lot of
    b. a lot more of
    c. a lot more
    d. many more

6. "Parachute jumping is a lot of fun."

    "But it must be _____ to jump for the first time."

    a. frightening
    b. fearful
    c. scaring
    d. frightened

7. "Those ceramic vases are attractive."

   "We saw _____ at the art fair."

   a. them being made   c. they being made
   b. make them   d. making them

8. "Why can't I eat?"

   "At no time _____ in the library."

   a. is permitted eating   c. is eating permitted
   b. eating it is permitted   d. eating is permitted

9. "Did you get your high school diploma?"

   "No, I didn't. But I wish I _____."

   a. had   c. will have
   b. were   d. will

10. "Lucy dyed her hair orange."

    "_____ it is a mystery to me."

    a. Why she did do it   c. Why she did
    b. Why did she   d. Why did she do it

11. "That antique desk is exactly what I need."

    "Would you consider _____ it?"

    a. buy   c. to buy
    b. buying   d. about buying

12. "Can I help you?"

    "Yes. Do you know _____?"

    a. when comes the bus   c. when will come the bus
    b. when does the bus come   d. when the bus comes

13. "Did Sue explain the math problems to you?"

    "Yes. Now I _____ them better."

    a. understanding   c. understand
    b. understood   d. had understood

14. "Fran needed a ride to the airport this morning."

    "If she had told me, I _____ her."

    a. would have drove   c. would have driven
    b. would had drove   d. would drive

15. "Do you think Barbara speaks Spanish well?"

    "She should. She _____ it since she was in high school."

    a. has been studying   c. is studying
    b. has studying   d. had been studying

16. "New York is a fascinating city."

    "_____ live there."

    a. So interesting people   c. Such interesting people
    b. Such interesting peoples   d. So many interesting peoples

17. "What did you think of Frank's new project?"

    "The more we heard about it, _____ we got."

    a. more enthusiastic   c. more enthusiasm
    b. the more enthusiastic   d. the most enthusiastic

18. "What did you do last night?"

    "I _____ tickets to the hockey game but decided to stay home instead."

    a. could get   c. could has gotten
    b. could have gotten   d. could to get

19. "Do we need more paper plates for the party?"

    "No. They _____."

    a. have already bought   c. had been bought already
    b. have been bought yet   d. have already been bought

20. "How was the magic show?"

    "It was _____."

    a. surprising entertaining   c. surprisingly entertaining
    b. surprisingly entertained   d. surprisingly entertainment

21. "Did Dan ask you where to get a bus schedule?"

    "I suggested _____ the bus station."

    a. he call   c. him to call
    b. he calling   d. he called

22. "Do you prefer jazz or rock music?"

    "I dislike _____ to music in general."

    a. to listen   c. listen
    b. listening   d. my listening

23. "Is your science project ready?"

    "No, and _____ it today, I won't pass the course."

    a. unless I finish   c. if I will finished
    b. unless I finished   d. if I finish

24. "Did you study last night?"

    "No. _____, I would have done better on today's test."

    a. Otherwise   c. If not
    b. Unless   d. If I hadn't

25. "How are your classes?"

    "I'm _____ ever."

    a. more busy than
    b. busier than

    c. more busier than
    d. busier that

26. "Are earthquakes common in this region?"

    "Almost never _____."

    a. do they occur
    b. they do occur

    c. they occur
    d. are they occurring

27. "I'm really hungry."

    "There are _____ cheese sandwiches on the table."

    a. a little
    b. a few

    c. a few of
    d. some of

28. "Why did you walk here?"

    "I let my daughter _____ my car to her friend's."

    a. driven
    b. drove

    c. drive
    d. to drive

29. "Can the doctor see me today?"

    "She's pretty busy. I'll ask her _____."

    a. how much time does she have
    b. how much time she has

    c. how much time she have
    d. how much time does she has

30. "Would you like to go to the movies tomorrow?"

    "Sure. By then I _____ my exam."

    a. will have finished
    b. will finished

    c. finished
    d. have finish

31. "Is this your hometown?"

    "No. I've only lived here _____."

    a. a few years ago
    b. for a few years

    c. since a few years
    d. until a few years

32. "Do you like living alone?"

    "Yes, and now I _____ for myself."

    a. used to cook
    b. am used to cooking

    c. used to cooking
    d. am used to cook

33. "I heard you had an appendix attack."

    "Yes. I _____ in the hospital until yesterday."

    a. must stay
    b. must have stayed

    c. have to stay
    d. had to stay

34. "Maybe the waiter will bring us some water to drink."

    "I wish he _____."

    a. will   c. would
    b. brings it   d. does

35. "What musical instrument does Irene play?"

    "Several, but she's famous _____ her piano playing."

    a. by   c. for
    b. about   d. to

36. "Do you ever go out dancing?"

    "I _____, but I quit."

    a. used to do   c. used to doing it
    b. used to   d. used

37. "The cake is gone."

    "_____ eaten it?"

    a. Could you   c. May you
    b. Might you   d. Might you have

38. "What did you think of that mystery you were reading?"

    "It wasn't _____."

    a. terrible excited   c. terrible exciting
    b. terribly exciting   d. terribly excited

39. "Where's the laundry?"

    "It _____ to the dry cleaner."

    a. has been taking   c. was took
    b. has taken   d. has been taken

40. "Do you think your father will worry if we're late?"

    "Maybe we'd better _____ him."

    a. call   c. to call
    b. should call   d. will call

Answer Key

— Unit 1: Nouns —

Pretest, p. 1

1. much homework (*homework* is noncount)
2. much knowledge (*knowledge* is noncount)
3. a cup of sugar (*sugar* is noncount)
4. How much (*money* is noncount)
5. a few (*hamburgers* is count)
6. much more research (*research* is noncount)
7. Fewer (*people* is count; irregular plural)
8. A large number (*clothes* is count)
9. much too much (*baggage* is noncount; *much* can precede *too much* for emphasis but it cannot precede *too many*)
10. How many (*tomatoes* is count)

Exercise, p. 3

1. d (*equipment* is noncount; it cannot be followed by -*s*)
2. c (*tornadoes* is count; *fewer of* cannot be directly followed by a noun)
3. b (*news* is noncount, even though it ends in -*s*)
4. a (*deer* is count; irregular plural)
5. b (*homework* is noncount)
6. a (*people* is count; irregular plural; *few* occurs with *ever*)
7. d (*trouble* is noncount)
8. c (*chocolate* is noncount; *so little* refers to *chocolate*)
9. c (*paint* is noncount here; *much of* cannot be directly followed by a noun)
10. b (*meat* is noncount)
11. a (*people* is count; irregular plural)
12. c (*coffee* is noncount)
13. a (*information* is noncount)
14. b (*fish* is count; irregular plural)
15. d (*wood* is noncount here)

Pretest, p. 5

1. I some information (*information* is noncount and cannot be preceded by *an*)
2. I important (adjectives are not pluralized before plural nouns in English)
3. I children (irregular plural)
4. C (*meter* functions as an adjective and is not pluralized)
5. I an (the *h* is silent in *hour*)
6. I person; everyone (*people* is plural, and *every* is used only with singular count nouns)
7. I each section (*each* is used only with singular count nouns)
8. C (*mathematics* functions as an adjective; the noun ends in -*s*)
9. I attractions (plural)
10. C (*the* is used to refer to a category of animals)

Exercise, p. 8

1. I message (adjectives are not pluralized in English)
2. C (*failure* is count)
3. I other (*another* occurs with singular count nouns)
4. I feet (irregular plural)
5. C (*every* is used with singular nouns)
6. I tourists (plural)
7. C
8. I all (occurs with the plural noun *questions*, which isn't necessary to include)
9. I holidays (plural)
10. C
11. I news stories (*many* occurs with the plural noun *stories*)
12. I The car industry (unique reference)
13. I guns; a gun (*gun* is count)

14. I   This year's interest rates (*year* is singular)
15. I   American women (irregular plural)
16. I   fruit and vegetables (here *fruit* is noncount; *vegetables* is count)
17. I   the importance of (*the* commonly occurs with *of*)
18. I   an extremely dangerous disease (*disease* is singular count)
19. C   (*the* refers back to an object, *hose,* which was previously mentioned)
20. I   the tire (*the* is used as a unique or specific reference)

Final Test, p. 9

1. C   (*the attic* is likely known by both speakers or is considered a part of a whole object, a house)
2. C   (*apples* is count)
3. I   a small amount of corn (*amount* occurs with noncount *corn*)
4. C
5. C
6. I   a little chalk; a few pieces of chalk (*chalk* is noncount)
7. I   other (*another* does not occur with plural count nouns)
8. I   The future of (*the* often occurs with *of*)
9. I   an invitation (*an* precedes count nouns beginning with a vowel sound)
10. I   one more piece of wood; one more board (*wood* is noncount)
11. I   many uses
12. C
13. C   (*mathematics* is noncount)
14. I   each section; all sections
15. C   (*dog* is used as a category of animals)

— Unit 2: Agreement —

Pretest, p. 11

1. is (*statistics* is noncount)
2. approves (*approves* agrees with *one*)
3. were (*were* agrees with *wishes*)
4. has (*the number of* agrees with *has*)
5. are (*are* agrees with *students*)
6. is (*is* agrees with *study*)
7. seems (*seems* agrees with *pediatrician*)
8. are (*are* agrees with *what you eat* and *how much you exercise*)
9. grow (*grow* agrees with *farmers*)
10. are (*are* agrees with *people*)

Exercise 1, p. 13

1. was (agrees with *courage*)
2. are (agrees with *tests*)

3. leaves (agrees with *one*)
4. is (agrees with *news*)
5. were (agrees with *amounts*)
6. was (agrees with *discussion*)
7. look (agrees with *both the table and the chair*)
8. have (agrees with *sheep;* irregular plural)
9. is (agrees with *that so many houses are being put up for sale*)
10. was (agrees with *singer*)
11. is (agrees with *one*)
12. was (agrees with *boat*)
13. reveal (agrees with *teeth;* irregular plural)
14. has (agrees with *capital city*)
15. was (agrees with *what the cooks prepared for dinner*)
16. is (agrees with *milk;* noncount)
17. are (agrees with *fish;* irregular plural)
18. are (agrees with *chances*)
19. don't (agrees with *bottles*)
20. is (agrees with *where the Olympic Games will be held*)

Exercise 2, p. 13

1. a (agrees with *everyone*)
2. b (agrees with *money;* noncount)
3. a (agrees with *fish;* irregular plural)
4. a (agrees with *children*)
5. b (agrees with *bowls*)
6. a (agrees with *the bedroom*)
7. a (agrees with *the number*)
8. b (agrees with *food*)
9. b (agrees with *trails*)
10. a (agrees with *economics;* noncount)

Pretest, p. 15

1. me (object pronoun after preposition *between*)
2. themselves (reflexive; *theirselves* is not a word in English)
3. itself (reflexive)
4. them (agrees with *reasons*)
5. her (refers to a woman, *Julia;* clue: the name ends in -*a*)
6. it is (obligatory subject pronoun *it*)
7. its (refers to *state*)
8. The cactus (the subject pronoun *it* is redundant)
9. Ours (refers to *we*)
10. she (subject pronoun)

Exercise, p. 16

1. I   its (refers to *horse*)
2. C   (*Robert* is a man's name)
3. I   himself (*hisself* is not a word in English)
4. C   (*her* refers to Sandra, a woman)
5. I   its (refers to *Earth*)

6. I (*they* is redundant and should be removed)
7. C
8. C (*Roberta* is a woman's name)
9. I himself/herself (*themselves* is used in conversational English)
10. C (it refers to *jewelry;* noncount)
11. I it is (obligatory subject pronoun)
12. I themselves (*theirselves* is not a word in English)
13. I yourselves (refers to two people)
14. I with them (object pronoun)
15. I between you and me (object pronoun)

Final Test, p. 17

1. C (*has* agrees with *that the committee members cannot agree with each other*)
2. C
3. C
4. I has been (agrees with *talk*)
5. C
6. I his (refers to *every boy; their* is sometimes used informally)
7. C (agrees with *basket*)
8. I has (agrees with *report*)
9. I (*it* is redundant)
10. I her (*Lisa* is a woman)

— Review Test, p. 18 —

1. another (*other*)
2. indicate (*indicates;* agrees with *rise*)
3. tooths (*teeth*)
4. world of politics (*the world of politics*)
5. much (*many*)
6. plant (*plants*)
7. is (*it is*)
8. a (omit *a; weather* is noncount)
9. pocket (*a pocket; pocket* is count)
10. two-weeks (*two-week*)

— Unit 3: Verb Tense —

Pretest, p. 19

1. is starting (present progressive; at this moment)
2. Do you understand (correct form; also *understand* generally occurs in the simple form of the verb)
3. like (simple present; fact)
4. came (simple past with *ago;* specific time in the past)
5. haven't finished (correct form; present perfect; began in the past but is still unfinished)
6. had had (past perfect; there is another past time reference, *before New Year's*)

7. has worked (present perfect with *for* + duration of time)
8. watched (list of activities in the simple past)
9. had arrived (past perfect; there is another past time reference)
10. will have sold (future perfect; with *by,* meaning *before*)
11. have finally finished (present perfect; indefinite past)
12. yet (present perfect; uncompleted action; *yet* used with negative)
13. for (duration of time)
14. since (specific time in the past)
15. Had you (correct form; past perfect; there is another past time reference)
16. has been giving (with *for;* started in the past and is still going on)
17. have (present)
18. know (*know* usually occurs in the simple form of the verb)
19. began (past; probably refers to *this morning*)
20. I'd seen (correct form; past perfect; there is another past time reference)

Exercise 1, p. 22

1. c (present perfect; indefinite past, *just*)
2. c (simple past; completed action)
3. b (simple present)
4. d (simple past; completed action)
5. a (present perfect progressive; began in the past and continues)
6. d (future perfect with *by* meaning *before*)
7. c (present perfect; indefinite past; *already*)
8. b (present perfect; began in the past and continues; *since*)
9. a (future perfect; with *by* meaning *before*)
10. c (simple past action)

Exercise 2, p. 24

1. b (past perfect; *when* means *before* in this sentence)
2. c (past perfect; there is another past time reference, *before you took it*)
3. c (present perfect; indefinite past; *already*)
4. d (simple past; completed action)
5. b (simple past; completed action)
6. b (past perfect progressive; there is another past time reference, *I got sick*)
7. b (present perfect; started in the past and is ongoing; *since*)
8. a (simple past; completed action; *ago*)
9. b (present perfect; *for*)
10. a (present perfect; negative; *yet*)

11. a (simple past)
12. b (simple past; short answer)
13. a (present perfect; irregular past participle; *begun, just*)
14. b (present perfect progressive; *for*)
15. c (simple present; semipermanent state?)

Final Test, p. 25

1. I   has (simple present; fact)
2. C   (simple past; completed action)
3. I   have visited (*visited* is the past participle)
4. I   died (simple past; completed action; past event)
5. I   died (simple past; completed action; past event)
6. I   played (parallel structure; actions in the past)
7. I   did not bring (negative form of the past tense)
8. I   has been (present perfect; began in the past and continues; *since*)
9. I   reigned (simple past; specific time in the past)
10. I   condenses (simple present; fact)

— Unit 4: Passive Voice —

Pretest, p. 27

1. c (passive voice; *caught* is an irregular past participle)
2. c (passive voice; present progressive; at this moment)
3. a (passive voice)
4. d (passive voice; *sent* is an irregular past participle)
5. a (active voice)

Exercise, p. 29

1. c (passive voice; past event)
2. a (passive voice; present perfect; *yet*)
3. d (passive voice; present perfect; *for*)
4. a (active voice; present perfect; *since*)
5. d (passive voice; completed action)
6. b (passive voice; past)
7. b (active voice; future perfect; *before*)
8. a (passive voice; past event; past time reference; *in the nineteenth century*)
9. a (passive voice)
10. c (passive voice; future; *will*)
11. a (present perfect; over time; up to the present)
12. d (present perfect; from past; the beginning of the week to now)
13. c (active voice; past event)
14. b (passive voice; *sent* is the irregular past participle)
15. a (active voice; past; definite time reference; *last night*)

Final Test, p. 31

1. I   have been indicated (past participle; *indicated*)
2. C
3. I   was founded (*founded* means *established*)
4. I   is sent (irregular past participle; *sent*)
5. I   It is recognized (passive voice)
6. C
7. I   is wasted (passive voice; past participle; *wasted*)
8. I   dropped (*drop* occurs in active voice)
9. C   (passive voice with modal; *can*)
10. I   was carried out (passive voice; past tense)

— Review Test, p. 32 —

1. applied (*is applied;* passive)
2. have increased (*has increased;* agrees with *the number*)
3. composed (*is composed;* passive)
4. has reelected (*was reelected;* passive)
5. has been (*had been; was*)
6. didn't brought (*didn't bring;* past tense; negative)
7. spend (*spent;* irregular past participle)
8. are fertilizing (*fertilize;* parallel structure; habitual action)
9. had never returned (*never returned;* simple past; *came . . . never returned*)
10. is still being used (*are;* agrees with *gadgets*)

— Unit 5: Modals —

Pretest, p. 33

1. a (*may* + V; possibility)
2. c (*ought* + to + V; expectation)
3. c (*are to* + V; requirement)
4. c (sense of obligation)
5. c (refusal)
6. d (past; recognition of error in judgment)
7. c (past; habitual; item d would be correct only with the addition of the object pronoun *it: used to do **it***)
8. b (past preference)
9. b (past of *will*)
10. b (past; would have been a possibility; also see unit 15)

Exercise 1, p. 37

1. b (past; obligation)
2. b (past of *have to;* necessity)
3. d (sense of obligation)
4. c (expectation)
5. a (past; possibility/conjecture)
6. d (expectation; *ought* + to + V)
7. a (obligation)

8. a (past habit; short answer; *used to play; used to do **it***)
9. a (past of *can;* ability)
10. a (habitual or repeated action in the past)

Exercise 2, p. 38

1. a (*would rather* + V; preference)
2. a (obligation)
3. c (future possibility)
4. c (willingness; offer)
5. a (future possibility)
6. a (necessity; *have + to* + V)
7. c (past; would have been a possibility; also see unit 15)
8. d (conclusion; past)
9. c (*would* + V; request)
10. c (future possibility; no verb required after *might*)

Final Test, p. 39

1. I   must be (*must* + V)
2. C   (*is + to* + V; future plan)
3. I   must have been (*must + have* + past participle)
4. I   used to run (*to* + V)
5. C   (future)
6. I   may change (future possibility)
7. I   would rather have gone (past unfulfilled preference)
8. C
9. C   (passive; possibility)
10. I   may surprise (*may* + V; *maybe the results . . . will surprise*)

— Unit 6:
Adjectives and Adverbs —

Pretest, p. 40

1. honest (adjective; modifies noun *opinion*)
2. clearly (adverb; modifies verb *thinking*)
3. certain (adjective; modifies the *that* clause)
4. directly (adverb; modifies verb *give*)
5. relatively (adverb; modifies adverb *well*)
6. thorough (adjective; modifies noun *inspection*)
7. really strange (adverb; modifies adjective *strange; real* is used in conversation)
8. scientifically (adverb; modifies *proven;* past participle)
9. seemingly honest (*seemingly* is an adverb; modifies adjective *honest*)
10. English so well (order; adverbs are not normally placed between the verb and the direct object)

Exercise 1, p. 42

1. slowly (adverb modifying *move*)
2. probable (adjective modifying the *that* clause)

3. beautifully (adverb modifying *dressed;* past participle)
4. strange (adjective used after the verb of perception *taste*)
5. the dessert so quickly (adverbs generally are not placed between the verb and the direct object)
6. fully (adverb modifying *aware*)
7. well (adverb modifying *running*)
8. comparatively (adverb modifying *new*)
9. heavily (adverb modifying *built;* past participle)
10. external (adjective modifying *use*)

Exercise 2, p. 42

1. a (adverb + adjective)
2. d (adverb + comparative adjective)
3. b (adverb + adjective)
4. b (adverb; modifies *speaking*)
5. d (adverb + comparative adjective)
6. b (adverb + adverb)
7. b (adjective + *and* + adjective)
8. b (adverb + adjective)
9. a (adverb + adjective)
10. c (adverb + adverb)

Final Test, p. 43

1. I   easily (modifies *move*)
2. C   (*unlikely* is an adjective)
3. I   Carefully controlled (adverb + past participle)
4. C   (adverb + past participle)
5. I   carefully and quickly (parallel structure; adverbs modify the verb *work*)
6. I   perfect score
7. I   narrowly escaped (adverb occurs before the verb, rather than between the verb and the object)
8. I   a hard metal (*hardly* is an adverb)
9. C
10. I   badly constructed car (adverb + past participle)

— Review Test, p. 45 —

1. individual (*individually* + past participle)
2. maybe (*may be*)
3. constantly (*constant*)
4. proper (*properly;* modifies the verb *dress*)
5. failed probably (*probably failed*)
6. should not to (*should not*)
7. quickly (*quick;* modifies the noun *promotion*)
8. soon (*soon present*)
9. are giving (*are being given;* passive)
10. been replaced (*being replaced;* present progressive; passive voice)

— Unit 7: Comparisons —

Pretest, p. 46

1. taller (comparative; compares two people)
2. than (*more . . . than*)
3. the same age as (*the same . . . as*)
4. the quieter (comparative; compares two people)
5. from (*different + from*)
6. ever (with superlatives)
7. less friendly (*less* cannot be combined with *more* or *-ier*)
8. the colder it got (*the* + comparative, *the* + comparative)
9. Of (*of* + the group of entities being compared; superlative)
10. Like (comparison of two named entities; points out similarity)
11. in contrast (contrast connector)
12. on the other hand (contrast connector; correct form)

Exercise 1, p. 50

1. most beautiful (superlative)
2. more slowly (comparative adverb)
3. the better (*the* + comparative, *the* + comparative)
4. than (comparative + *than*)
5. a lot more (comparative + *than*)
6. as tall as (similarity; *as* + adjective + *as*)
7. the same (similarity; the same + noun + *as*)
8. alike (meaning *similar;* adjective)
9. ever (used with superlatives)
10. on the other hand (contrast connector; correct form)
11. while (connects two clauses within a sentence)
12. in contrast (connects two sentences separated by a semicolon or period)

Exercise 2, p. 50

1. c (*of* + the group of entities being compared; superlative)
2. a (comparative)
3. b (comparative)
4. b (comparison of two mentioned entities; points out similarity)
5. c (superlative)
6. c (*different* + from)
7. b (*the* + comparative, *the* + comparative)
8. c (superlative; three entities are being compared)
9. b (*the* + comparative, *the* + comparative)
10. b (comparative; only two entities are being compared)

Final Test, p. 52

1. I   biggest (*big* is one syllable)
2. C
3. I   much more snow than (*more . . . than*)
4. C
5. I   less high (*less* cannot occur with *more* or *-ier*)
6. I   the smaller
7. C
8. I   warmer than; as warm as
9. I   as many calories (*so* may be used with a verb in the negative)
10. I   like

— Unit 8: Adjectives Ending in *-ing* and *-ed* —

Pretest, p. 53

1. disappointing (characterizes the scores; they caused disappointment)
2. Scared (the hikers' response)
3. delightful (characterizes the dessert)
4. overwhelming (characterizes the task)
5. surprised (the people's response; effect on the people)

Exercise, p. 55

1. c (Margaret's response)
2. b (characterizes the circus)
3. d (my response)
4. a (characterizes the musical)
5. b (our response to the news)
6. a (characterizes the class)
7. c (characterizes the news)
8. a (characterizes the infinitive *to see such quality*)
9. a (Monica's response to the scooter; its effect on her)
10. d (my response to the thunder)

Final Test, p. 56

1. I   frightening (characterizes the statistics)
2. C
3. C
4. I   boring (characterizes the winters)
5. I   delightful (correct form)

— Review Test, p. 57 —

1. alike (*like;* compares two similar, mentioned entities)
2. scary (*scared;* effect)
3. most great (*greatest; great* is a one-syllable adjective)
4. bestest (*best; bestest* is not a word in English)

5. more as (*more than*)
6. less healthier (*less healthy*)
7. as same (*the same*)
8. excited (*exciting;* characterizes New York)
9. Whereas (*In contrast; However; whereas* cannot be used to connect two sentences)
10. in the other hand (*on the other hand*)

— Unit 9: *So and Such* —

Pretest, p. 58

1. d (*such* + noun phrase; *person* is singular count)
2. a (*so* + adjective)
3. a (*so* + adjective)
4. a (*such* + noun phrase; *trouble* is noncount)
5. c (*so* + adjective + *that* + result)

Exercise, p. 60

1. b (*such* + noun phrase; *day* is count)
2. c (*so* + adjective)
3. a (*so* + adjective + *a/an* + count noun; less frequent than *such an important person* but similar in meaning)
4. a (*so much;* quantity expression; *money* is noncount; see unit 1)
5. d (*such* + noun phrase; *people* is a plural count noun)
6. b (*so much* + *that;* result; *much* modifies the verb *like*)
7. c (*such* + noun phrase; *clothes* is plural)
8. d (*so very* + adjective; *very* adds emphasis)

Final Test, p. 61

1. C
2. C
3. I   such a (word order)
4. C
5. I   so lightweight (*so* + adjective)

— Unit 10: Word Classification —

Throughout, an asterisk (*) following a word indicates that the word does not exist in English.

Pretest, p. 62

1. economical (cost saving)
2. entry (noun)
3. imported (*importationed**)
4. musicians (people; *musical* refers to a theatrical production with songs)
5. delay (*delayance**)
6. professional (adjective modifying *use*)
7. documentary (*documental**)
8. disturbance (*disturb* is a verb)

9. aristocratic (*aristocratical**)
10. equality (*equalness**)

List 1—Verbs and nouns, p. 64

definition	prevention
delay	prohibition
equipment	purchase
establishment	recognition
expectation	reduction
an import/importation	request
an indication/indicator	resignation
investment	sale
isolation	start
measurement	surprise
need	survival
opposition	a transformation/transformer

List 2—Adjectives and nouns, p. 64

ease	prevalence
familiarity	responsibility
happiness	suitability
humidity	tradition
jealousy	urgency
length	warmth

Exercise, p. 65

1. I   clear (parallel structure; three adjectives)
2. I   invaded (*invasion* is a noun)
3. I   authorities (*authorization* means permission)
4. C
5. I   depth (*deepness**)
6. I   sculptor (*sculpture* refers to an object)
7. I   security (parallel structure; three nouns)
8. C
9. I   fool (*foolish* is an adjective; *fool* is a count noun)
10. I   construction (*construct* is usually a verb)
11. I   confident (parallel structure; three adjectives)
12. I   Well-operated (*operation* is a noun; not a past participle)
13. I   dance (parallel structure; the noun *dance,* rather than the gerund *dancing,* accompanies the other three nouns; it is possible to imagine a sentence with three gerunds: *acting, dancing, drawing*)
14. I   dependability (*dependableness**)
15. I   persistent (*persistence* is a noun)

Final Test, p. 65

1. restricts (*restrictions;* noun)
2. necessitates (*necessities; necessitates* is a verb)
3. scientifics* (*scientists;* noun)

4. searchings* (*searches;* noun)
5. alternations (*alternatives;* means choices)
6. salty (*salt;* noun; parallel structure)
7. marriage (*married;* past participle)
8. threatenings* (*threats;* noun)
9. air-condition (*air-conditioned;* adjective; *air-condition* is a verb)
10. lightly (*light;* adjective; *bubbly* is an adjective)

— Review Test, p. 67 —

Test 1

1. never (*ever*)
2. athletics (*athletes,* which refers to people; *athletics* is the discipline)
3. contributes (*contributions;* noun)
4. safety (*safe;* parallel structure; three adjectives)
5. simpleness* (*simplicity*)
6. protection (*protect;* verb)

Test 2

1. a (*so* + adjective)
2. a (*such* + noun phrase; *weather* is noncount)
3. d (*so many;* quantity expression + plural count noun)
4. a (*such* + noun phrase; *food* is noncount)

— Unit 11: Prepositions —

Pretest, p. 69

1. a (*insist on*)
2. a (*opposed to*)
3. b (*responsible for*)
4. a (*impression of*)
5. c (*faced with*)

Exercise 1, p. 70

1. d (*distinguish* X *from* Y)
2. b (*believe in*)
3. c (*apologize for*)
4. c (*graduate from*)
5. d (*complain about*)
6. b (*base on*)
7. d (*depend on*)
8. b (*mean by*)
9. a (*prefer* X *to* Y)
10. b (*combine with*)
11. a (*dream of* or *about*)
12. d (*award to*)
13. d (*insist on*)
14. a (*consist of*)
15. a (*contribute to*)

Exercise 2, p. 72

1. C
2. I (*apply to*)
3. C
4. I (*operate on*)
5. I (*approve of*)
6. I (*worry about*)

Exercise 3, p. 73

1. d (*filled with*)
2. b (*married to*)
3. a (*composed of*)
4. a (*associate with*)
5. a (*worried about*)
6. a (*familiar with*)
7. a (*famous for*)
8. d (*allergic to*)
9. d (*jealous of*)
10. a (*thankful for*)
11. d (*interested in*)
12. d (*tired of*)

Exercise 4, p. 75

1. I (*bored with*)
2. I (*angry at;* anger directed at someone)
3. C
4. I (*afraid of*)
5. I (*fond of*)

Exercise 5, p. 77

1. a (*on* + day)
2. a (*in* + month)
3. c (*on* + date)
4. a (*at* + noon)
5. b (*on* + street)
6. d (*at* + street address)
7. d (opposite of *to*)
8. b (*between* X *and* Y)
9. c (*scar on;* not *in, inside*)
10. d (*from* time *to* time; expression)
11. c (*prior* + *to*)
12. d (*At the beginning* refers to when the meeting opens)
13. a (*in the corner* refers to a corner inside a structure)
14. b (*on the corner* refers to a corner outside)
15. a (*at* + *night*)
16. a (*during* + *the night*)
17. c (*close* + *to*)
18. a (*for* + duration of time; see unit 3)
19. b
20. b

— Unit 12: Gerunds and Infinitives —

Pretest, p. 81

1. Learning (V + -ing; gerund in subject position)
2. doing (enjoy + gerund)
3. about running (thinking + preposition about + gerund)
4. Your (possessive before gerund)
5. going (preposition without + gerund)
6. not smoking (negative form of the gerund)
7. washing (get used to + gerund; to is a preposition)
8. by requesting (means; preposition by + gerund)
9. being robbed (gerund; passive construction)
10. defeat (noun + of)

Exercise, p. 84

1. a (worry about + gerund; gerund after prepositions)
2. c (possessive noun + gerund)
3. b (look forward to + gerund; to is a preposition)
4. c (possessive before gerund; to is a preposition)
5. c
6. a
7. b (means; preposition by + gerund)
8. d (the verb consider is not followed by a preposition; your is redundant)
9. c (adjective tired + of + gerund)
10. b (led to + possessive + gerund; to is a preposition)
11. c (noun explanation is used instead of the gerund; explaining would be used if an object followed)
12. d (am used to + gerund; to is a preposition)
13. c (passive construction)
14. a (passive construction)
15. c

Pretest, p. 88

1. to visit (encourage + to + V; infinitive)
2. to take (possible + to + V)
3. to do (nothing left + to + V)
4. not to sell (negative; not + to + V)
5. you to bring (you + to + V)
6. To make bread (in order to; purpose)
7. rebuild (parallel structure; to + V, (to) + V; the second to is optional)
8. to put
9. cleaning (gerund; or to be cleaned; doer unknown)
10. to be examined (passive construction)

Exercise, p. 88

1. c (afford + to + V)
2. b (encourage + object pronoun + to + V)

3. a (the first, the second + to + V)
4. b (not before an infinitive)
5. a (infinitive in subject position; thus preceded by for + object pronoun)
6. c
7. c (dislike + gerund)
8. d (like + to + V)
9. b
10. c (lucky + to + V; passive)
11. c (get + to + V)
12. c (want + to + V; passive)
13. c (parallel structure; means; by + gerund)
14. b (in order to; purpose)
15. a (plan + to + V)

Pretest, p. 90

1. a (make + V)
2. a (let + V)
3. c (have + V)
4. a (hear + present participle [V + -ing]; verb of perception; action in progress)
5. d (see + past participle; verb of perception + past participle; passive form)

Exercise, p. 92

1. c (have + V)
2. b (made + V)
3. b (verb of perception + present participle; action in progress)
4. a (let + V)
5. b (possible + to + V)
6. a (have + past participle; passive construction)
7. c (verb of perception + past participle; passive construction)
8. a (have + V)
9. b (get + to + V)
10. b (have + V; imperative)

Exercise 1, p. 93

1. b (make + V)
2. a (first + to + V)
3. c (forward to + gerund)
4. b (tired of + gerund)
5. b (used to + gerund; passive construction)
6. c (possible + for + me + to + V)
7. d (to + V in the passive)
8. c (possessive noun before gerund)
9. b (be used to + gerund)
10. d (have + V)
11. c (in order to; purpose)
12. a (in order to; purpose)
13. a (dislike + gerund)

14. b (noun)
15. c (*for* + gerund; purpose)

Exercise 2, p. 95

1. d (*want* + *to* + V)
2. d (parallel structure; means)
3. c (verb of perception; passive; progressive)
4. b (preposition *to* + gerund)
5. d
6. a
7. b (*insist on* + gerund)
8. d (*think about* + gerund)
9. a (*consider* + gerund)
10. d (*lead to* + possessive + gerund)

Final Test, p. 96

1. I   (*relaxing*)
2. I   (*not to eat*)
3. C
4. I   (*about retiring*)
5. I   (*the preparation*)
6. I   (*to go*)
7. C
8. I   (*to inform*)
9. C
10. C

— Review Test, p. 98 —

Test 1

1. for construct (*to construct, to* + V; *for constructing, for* + gerund)
2. identify (*identifying; led to our* + gerund)
3. to enter (*from entering; prevent from* + gerund)
4. making (*to make*; parallel structure; *to reduce as well as to make*)
5. speed (*speeding; prevent from* + gerund)

Test 2

1. b (*be faced with*)
2. a (*interested in*)
3. b (*depend on*)
4. a (*persuade* someone + *to* + V)
5. b (*in* + year)

— Unit 13: *That* Clauses and Interrogative Clauses —

Pretest, p. 100

1. that (embedded *that* clause as object)
2. That the fire destroyed (embedded *that* clause as subject)
3. the guests are (embedded question; no inversion)

4. How many eggs a hen lays (embedded question; no inverted auxiliary)
5. whether or not (embedded yes-no question; *if or not* is not possible in English)

Exercise, p. 102

1. a (embedded *that* clause as subject)
2. a (embedded question; no inversion)
3. a (embedded question; no inverted auxiliary *does*)
4. b (embedded question; no inverted auxiliary *does*)
5. a (embedded yes-no question)
6. c (embedded yes-no question with *whether or not*)
7. b (embedded question; no inversion)
8. d (embedded question; no inversion)
9. c (embedded *that* clause as subject)
10. a (embedded question; no inversion; *whom* is formal)
11. a (embedded question; no inverted auxiliary)
12. a (embedded question; no inverted auxiliary)
13. b (embedded yes-no question as subject; only *whether* is permitted in subject position)
14. a (embedded question; no inversion)
15. b (embedded question; no inverted auxiliary)

Final Test, p. 103

1. C
2. I   whether or not
3. C
4. C
5. I   what you like (no subject-auxiliary inversion)

— Unit 14: Adjective (Relative) Clauses —

Pretest, p. 104

1. a (restricted adjective clause)
2. a (the sentence does not contain an adjective clause)
3. d (*whose* + noun; refers to Frida Kahlo; restricted adjective clause)
4. d (unrestricted adjective clause; *which* required rather than *that*)
5. c (reduced adjective clause; *which was* has been removed)
6. b (reduced adjective clause or appositive; *which is* has been removed)

Exercise, p. 107

1. b (restricted adjective clause; *that* refers to *substance*)
2. b (reduced adjective clause; *which was* has been removed)
3. a (*whose* + noun phrase)

4. b (reduced adjective clause)
5. b (reduced adjective clause; *which started* is dropped, and V + *-ing* takes its place)
6. c (restricted adjective clause)
7. b (restricted adjective clause; *store in*)
8. d (there is no adjective clause in this sentence)
9. b (unrestricted adjective clause)
10. c (reduced unrestricted adjective clause)

Final Test, p. 108

1. d (restricted adjective clause; definition; *apply with*)
2. b (unrestricted adjective clause)
3. d (reduced unrestricted adjective clause)
4. b (*whose* + noun phrase)
5. b (*that* can be omitted because it is the object pronoun in the adjective clause)
6. a (*responsible for;* some speakers may prefer *for whom*)
7. a (reduced restricted adjective clause)
8. a (reduced restricted adjective clause)

— Review Test, p. 110 —

1. a (*that have* is reduced to *having*)
2. d (restricted adjective clause; *that* or *who*)
3. b (embedded *that* clause in subject position)
4. d (interrogative clause; no subject-auxiliary inversion)
5. b (*whose* + noun; restricted adjective clause)
6. a (embedded yes-no question)
7. b (embedded *that* clause in subject position)
8. a (*at whose*)
9. a (reduced relative clause; *who knew* is reduced to *knowing*)
10. a (*with which;* alternative wording could be *a device clothes are made with*)

— Unit 15: *If* (Conditional) Clauses —

Pretest, p. 112

1. go (type 1; present tense in the *if* clause)
2. I'll be (type 1; *will* + V in the main clause)
3. were (type 2; past tense in the *if* clause; *were* instead of *was*)
4. would (type 2; *would* + V in the main clause)
5. have (type 3; *could* + *have* + past participle)
6. had (type 3; past perfect in the *if* clause)
7. should (type 1; *should* can be used in the *if* clause)
8. Should (type 1; inversion with *should*)
9. Were (type 2; inversion with *were*)
10. Had the committee members (type 3; inversion with *had*)

11. unless (negative form; similar to *if you don't promise*)
12. Call (there is no *if* clause in this sentence)

Exercise, p. 115

1. a (type 2; past tense in the *if* clause)
2. d (*otherwise* and *if not* have similar meanings)
3. b (type 3; *would* + *have* + past participle in the main clause)
4. a (type 2; *would* + V in the main clause)
5. d (type 1; present tense in the *if* clause)
6. d (type 3; past perfect in the *if* clause; passive)
7. b (type 3; *would* + *have* + past participle in the main clause)
8. d (type 2; past; *were* replaces *was* in the *if* clause)
9. a (type 3; inversion)
10. c (type 1; negative *unless*)
11. c (type 3; notice the short answer in the *if* clause; long form, *If I had needed help*)
12. a (this sentence does not have an *if* clause)
13. c (short form)
14. a (negative *unless*)
15. a (type 3; inversion)

Final Test, p. 117

1. I   it will (type 1; present tense in the main clause)
2. C
3. C
4. C
5. C

— Unit 16: Wish —

Pretest, p. 118

1. b (type 2; past; *was* changes to *were;* desire for the existence of something)
2. a (type 1; *would;* request)
3. d (type 3; past perfect; regret about the past)
4. b (type 1; *could;* desire to be able to do something)
5. c (type 3; past perfect; regret about the past)

Exercise, p. 120

1. a (type 2; desire for the existence of something)
2. d (type 3; regret about the past)
3. c (type 1; desired ability)
4. d (type 3; regret about the past)
5. a (type 2)
6. c (type 1; strong request)
7. a (type 3)
8. b (type 3; short answer for *had finished*)
9. d (type 1; short answer)
10. a (type 2; desire for a changed state)

Final Test, p. 121

1. I could do (type 1; *can* is not an option; only *could* and *would* are options)
2. C
3. I would cut down (type 1; present or past tense is not an option; only *would* and *could* are options)
4. C
5. I hadn't broken (type 3; present perfect is not an option; only past perfect is an option)

— Review Test, p. 122 —

1. a (type 3 *if* clause)
2. c (type 1 *if* clause; inversion with *should*)
3. a (*otherwise* means *if not* or *if they don't*)
4. d (type 3 *wish;* short answer; *had seen it*)
5. c (type 2 *if* clause)
6. b (this is not an *if* clause)
7. a (type 1 *wish;* desire for things to change)
8. a (type 3 *if* clause; inversion with *had*)
9. b (type 1 *wish*)
10. c (type 2 *wish*)

— Unit 17: Negative Adverbs —

Pretest, p. 124

1. b (*never again* + subject-*be* inversion)
2. d (*hardly ever* + subject; subject-auxiliary inversion)
3. d (*neither* + inversion)
4. b (*not until* + inversion)
5. a (*only recently* + inversion)

Exercise, p. 126

1. c (*never* + subject-auxiliary inversion)
2. a (*no sooner* + inversion)
3. c (*no longer* + inversion)
4. b (*as* + inversion of *do*)
5. c (*nowhere* + inversion)
6. a (*hardly ever* follows the subject *you* here; moreover, it cannot occur between the verb and object; see unit 6)
7. d (*at no time* + inversion)
8. d (*only* + inversion)
9. c (*nor* + subject-auxiliary inversion)
10. a (*not only* + subject-auxiliary inversion)

Final Test, p. 127

1. I are mosquitoes (*nowhere* + inversion)
2. C
3. I (*not until* + inversion)
4. C (there is no inversion in this sentence because *no longer* does not precede the subject)
5. C

— Unit 18: *That* Clauses in the Subjunctive (Bare Infinitive) —

Pretest, p. 128

1. d (*recommend* + *that* clause in the subjunctive; *rest* instead of *rests)*
2. a (*important* + *that* clause in the subjunctive; *do* instead of *does)*
3. d (*requested* + *that* clause in the subjunctive; *go* instead of *went* or *goes)*
4. b (*suggested* + *that* clause in the subjunctive; *take* instead of *takes* or *took)*
5. b (*insist on* + gerund; cf. *insist that* + subjunctive)

Exercise, p. 130

1. a (*urgent* + *that* clause in the subjunctive)
2. b (*recommend* + *that* clause in the subjunctive)
3. b (*necessary* + *that* clause in the subjunctive)
4. b (*surprising* is followed by a *that* clause but not a *that* clause in the subjunctive; see unit 13)
5. c (*insisted* + *that* clause in the subjunctive; *that* is optional; see list on p. 130)
6. b (*recommend* + *that* clause in the subjunctive)
7. c (*suggest* + *that* clause in the subjunctive; *that* is optional; see list on p. 130)
8. c (*insisted on* + gerund)
9. a (*it's possible* is followed by a *that* clause but not a *that* clause in the subjunctive; see unit 13)
10. c (here *asked* is followed by the infinitive rather than a *that* clause in the subjunctive; it is also possible to say, *I asked that she stop;* in this case, *that* is obligatory)

Final Test, p. 131

1. C (*not* is used before a verb in the subjunctive)
2. C
3. I repair (*that* clause in the subjunctive)
4. I that (*insist on* is followed by a gerund, not *that)*
5. C (*prefer* + *that* clause in the subjunctive)

— Review Test, p. 132 —

1. b (*seldom* + inverted auxiliary)
2. a (*suggest* + *that* clause in the subjunctive)
3. c (*only* + inversion)
4. a (*recommended* + *that* clause in the subjunctive)
5. a (*propose* + *that* clause in the subjunctive; bare infinitive *be* is used)
6. b (*neither* + inversion)
7. b (*never* + inversion)
8. a (*insisted on* + possessive + gerund; *insisted that we stay* has basically the same meaning)
9. d (*asked* + infinitive rather than *that* clause; both are possible)
10. a (*as* + subject-auxiliary inversion)

— Examinations —

Exam 1, p. 135

Part 1

1. d (*is* is the main verb; present tense)
2. a (*in* + decade)
3. b (superlative; *in* + location)
4. d (present progressive; passive)
5. a (reduced restricted adjective clause; *that are* has been omitted)
6. b (*the* + comparative, *the* + comparative)
7. c (type 1 *if* clause; simple present in the *if* clause)
8. a (*that* clause in subject position)
9. a (present perfect; *since;* passive)
10. d (simple present; negative)
11. b (*in* + century)
12. a (*only* + inversion)
13. b (*as* + subject-auxiliary inversion)
14. c (type 3 *if* clause)
15. a (restricted relative clause)

Part 2

1. to (remove *to*)
2. are (*is; clothing* is noncount)
3. availableness (*availability*)
4. painting (*painter*)
5. amount (*number; waterways* is count)
6. plant (*plants;* plural)
7. discover (*discovered;* past participle; passive voice)
8. a (*an; accomplishment* begins with a vowel)
9. to energy crisis (*to the energy crisis;* unique; known reference)
10. as (*than*)
11. from time and time (*from time to time*)
12. cautious (*caution;* noun)
13. lightly (*light*)
14. overcome (*overcame;* irregular past)
15. for going (*to go; permission* + *to* + V)
16. spoil (*to spoil; cause* + *to* + V)
17. river (*rivers;* plural)
18. feets (*feet;* irregular plural)
19. on (*of; consists* + *of*)
20. are paid (*is paid; income* is singular)
21. will move (*moves;* present tense in type 1 *if* clauses)
22. so (*as; as . . . as*)
23. to paint (*in painting; interest* + *in* + *painting*)
24. about (remove *about;* the verb *concern* is not followed by a preposition)
25. it (remove *it;* redundancy)

Exam 2, p. 138

1. d (*of* + the group of entities being compared; superlative)
2. c (adverb + adverb)
3. a (*recommend* + *that* clause in the subjunctive)
4. c (*the first* + *to* + V)
5. b (*have* + V)
6. a (characterizes the miniseries)
7. b (*need* + gerund)
8. d (*is* + *to* + V; modal; plan)
9. a (negative of *would rather; not* before V)
10. a (*concerns* + gerund)
11. d (present perfect progressive; *since*)
12. c (*such* + noun phrase; *people* is plural)
13. d (see unit 6 for an explanation of adverb placement)
14. d (*on the contrary* cannot be used here to show contrast)
15. a (adverb + adjective)
16. c (*be used to* + gerund; passive)
17. c (*the same . . . as*)
18. c (type 3 *wish;* short answer for *had ordered them*)
19. a (simple past; negative)
20. a (*so* + adjective; followed by *that* + result)
21. b (*ought* + *to;* modal)
22. c (*never* + inversion)
23. a (type 3 *if* clause; *had* inversion)
24. a (possessive + gerund in subject position)
25. a (present progressive; in progress)
26. d (*on* + date)
27. a (type 1 *if* clause; *should* inversion)
28. a (type 2 *wish*)
29. a (present progressive; passive)
30. a (modal *can* in the past; conjecture)
31. c (simple past; *ago*)
32. b (*have* + *to;* modal; necessity)
33. b (simple past; passive)
34. b (restricted adjective clause)
35. b (imperative; there is no *if* clause in this sentence)
36. b (past perfect; there is another past time reference)
37. a (*coins* is count)
38. b (*since* + a time in the past)
39. b (*so little* refers to *food,* which is noncount)
40. a (*that* clause in subject position)

Exam 3, p. 142

Part 1

1. c (parallel structure; *sorted* is the past participle; the second *are* has been eliminated; passive)
2. b (*by* meaning *before the beginning of*)
3. a (*operate* + *on*)

4. c (reduced restricted adjective clause; *that is* has been removed)
5. c (*species* is singular here; notice *one*)
6. a (there is no adjective clause in this sentence)
7. a (*the* is a unique reference)
8. b (past perfect; *until*)
9. a (*the* + comparative, *the* + comparative)
10. c (type 1 *if* clause; *should* inversion)
11. a (*whose* + noun phrase *cartoon characters; whose* refers to Walt Disney)
12. b (*nowhere* + inversion)
13. a (*not only* + subject-auxiliary inversion)
14. a (interrogative clause in object position; no inversion)
15. a (type 1 *if* clause; present tense in the *if* clause)

Part 2

1. attend (*to attend; encourage* + *to* + V)
2. significance (*significant;* adjective)
3. It estimated (*It is estimated;* obligatory *is*)
4. as (remove *as;* verb *consider* is not followed by a preposition)
5. conventionally (*conventional;* adjective)
6. ordinance (*ordinances;* plural)
7. a (*an; imported* begins with a vowel)
8. are measure (*are measured;* past participle; passive)
9. become (*became;* irregular form in the past)
10. elegance (*elegant;* parallel structure; list of adjectives)
11. pass (*passing;* gerund in subject position)
12. darkness (*dark;* adjective)
13. have (*has;* agrees with *topic*)
14. donates generously money (*generously donates money; generously* cannot be placed between the verb and the object)
15. educated (*educational;* adjective describing *materials; educated* describes people)
16. alike (*like;* comparison of two mentioned entities)
17. years (*year;* adjectives do not occur in the plural in English)
18. researches (*research;* noncount)
19. the (remove *the;* no unique or specific reference)
20. healthy (*health;* noun)
21. lose (*to lose; cause* + *to* + V)
22. be aware (*to be aware; for . . . to*)
23. relative (*relatively;* adverb modifying *inexpensive*)
24. had recently returned (*have recently returned;* present perfect; indefinite past; *recently*)
25. influenced (*influence;* parallel structure; *to shelter . . . , educate . . . , and influence*)

Exam 4, p. 145

1. b (present progressive; in progress)
2. b (*during* + *the afternoon*)
3. d (*homework* is noncount, but *assignments* is count)
4. b (adverb modifying *moving*)
5. c (comparative)
6. a (*frightening* characterizes *parachute jumping*)
7. a (verb of perception + present participle + past participle; passive construction)
8. c (*at no time* + inversion)
9. a (type 3 *wish;* past regret)
10. c (interrogative clause in subject position; no subject-auxiliary inversion)
11. b (*consider* + gerund)
12. d (interrogative clause; no inversion)
13. c (simple present; *now*)
14. c (type 3 *if* clause)
15. a (present perfect progressive; past to present; *since*)
16. c (*such* + noun phrase; *people* is plural)
17. b (*the* + comparative, *the* + comparative)
18. b (rejected possibility in the past)
19. d (present perfect; *already;* past indefinite)
20. c (adverb + adjective; *entertaining* characterizes *the magic show*)
21. a (*suggest* + *that* clause in the subjunctive; *that* is optional)
22. b (*dislike* + gerund)
23. a (negative *unless* appearing in type 1 *if* clause; present tense)
24. a (rather than if *I hadn't* because the speaker's response to the question is *no*)
25. b (comparative)
26. a (*almost never* + inversion)
27. b (*sandwiches* is plural count)
28. c (*let* + V; bare infinitive)
29. b (embedded interrogative clause; no inversion)
30. a (future perfect; *by then* meaning *before*)
31. b (*for* + duration)
32. b (*be used to* + gerund)
33. d (past necessity)
34. c (type 1 *wish*)
35. c (*famous for*)
36. b (past habit; short for *used to dance, used to do it*)
37. d (past possibility)
38. b (adverb + adjective; *exciting* characterizes *that mystery*)
39. d (past perfect; indefinite past; passive)
40. a (*had better* + V; modal)